Out of the Blue

Blue

The Life and Legend of Kirby "Sky King" Grant

TIM TROTT

Published by Tim Trott, Tim Trott Audio, Inc

This book is dedicated to the memory of Kirby "Sky King" Grant, who inspired a generation of pilots, instructors, air traffic controllers, and astronauts.

EDITED and REVISED

Revision 29 – May 30, 2024

Contents

About this Book

- Do you remember the Sky King TV show?

- Who flew the plane in the shows?

- Was Kirby Grant a "real" pilot?

- How many "Songbird" planes were there?

- What happened to the "missing episodes"?

- What did Kirby Grant do after the TV series ended?

- Did you know that Kirby Grant was a singer and concert violinist?

Those of us of a certain age grew up with the Sky King television show. Those old black and white TV shows inspired many aviation careers. That includes many airline pilots, flight instructors and even astronauts.

I met and got to know Kirby Grant and his wife, Carolyn, after they retired to Central Florida in 1971. I visited Kirby as he was recovering from heart surgery in 1978. He told me he was writing a book! The title would be the iconic words of the announcer at the opening of Sky King television shows. The title was to be "Out of the Blue". Kirby even mentioned the not-yet-started

book in an interview on Good Morning America. You can view that interview and others on my Tim Trott Productions YouTube channel.

After Kirby's passing in 1986, Carolyn Grant told me that "book" had existed only in Kirby's mind and intentions. Writing this book is the fulfillment of a promise I made to Carolyn Grant.

Bill Fergusson was a Cessna sales manager. He was the pilot who flew the Cessna 310B for the later series' flying sequences. Michael McMurtrey shared an interview he had with Bill.

I also got help ...and an *"I knew Sky King"* T-shirt... from Dale Fergusson, Bill Fergusson's wife, who once had a page on BlogSpot.com.

I must also express my appreciation to Amy and Steve Brown of Brown Flying School at the Sky King Airport. That airport is still in Carolyn Grant's hometown of Terre Haute, Indiana. They shared their memories and photographs of Kirby's many visits there. I also met Stearman stunt pilot Walter Pierce. Walter shared his memories and personal impressions of "Sky King." when they touring with Kirby in the Great American Air Show.

The original subtitle was "The Life and Times of Kirby 'Sky King' Grant". I realized Legend was more appropriate. And thus the title became "The Life and Legend of Kirby 'Sky King' Grant." The word "legend" is appropriate because of the mythology that surrounds the show. There are stories out there that are not true. I will clarify some of those myths in this book and I might even reveal a few secrets.

Legends tend to be a blend of fact and fiction. For example, we're pretty sure that Davy Crockett did not kill a bear as a toddler of 3. So, too, there are many conflicting references to Kirby Grant. One newspaper reported that Kirby Grant had died piloting his plane in 1986. His death actually occurred in a traffic accident in the previous year. Carolyn sent me a copy of that newspaper ad. You'll find a picture of it in the last chapter. That is only one of several instances where I found inconsistencies.

Kirby Grant wore his iconic white hat long past his acting days. He was true to the traditions that white hat symbolized in American Westerns. Kirby was the quintessential "good guy." He wore that hat to public appearances in his later life. I knew Kirby on a first-name basis but only met him a few times. I know him better after working on this book. I hope that you enjoy the story of the life and legend of Kirby "Sky King" Grant:

the TV hero of generations of aviators. Those pilots found inspiration in the 1950s television series.

I never got Kirby's autograph because I never asked. Somehow I never thought of it. You don't ask for autographs from friends, and that's how I thought of Kirby. He was a guest in my house, and I in his.

The Book Project

After Kirby died in October 1985, I contacted Carolyn Grant. She told me that the "book" Kirby had described only existed in his mind and intentions. Carolyn had moved to New Orleans to stay with a family friend, Larry Tate. I sent her a Radio Shack cassette recorder and a box of blank tapes. She recorded her thoughts and memories on the cassettes over several months. She mailed them back to me, along with newspaper clippings and other things, and we spoke on the phone. She recorded over six hours of material, which I transcribed and kept with my notes. Carolyn passed away a few years later in 1989, at age 61. As with Kirby, the "Out of the Blue" project was something I had intended to do, but had not quite gotten around to doing. But I kept meeting so many people inspired by Kirby Grant and the Sky King TV show.

Years later, I had completed writing a couple of e-Books, and I decided it was time to get back to the Sky King book project. As my wife pointed out, if I kept putting it off, everybody affected by Sky King would be gone. I searched for Kirby's son, Kip, and found a mailing address not far from where I used to live in Central Florida. I recalled meeting him when I visited their home after Kirby's heart surgery. I mailed Kip a DVD of a few of Kirby's TV interviews I had on VHS tape. He responded one Sunday night, and he invited me to meet with him on my next trip to Central Florida. I took him up on his offer and recorded an interview at his home, helping me to fill in some details.

Steve Brown and his wife still operate the flying school that Herman Brown began at Sky King Airport in Indiana. At the time I spoke with them, they were going to be camping in Illinois, so we met them there.

In my research, I found a a blog post by Dayle Fergusson.Dayle was the wife of the Cessna sales manager, the pilot of the Cessna 310B for the later episodes of the series. I also tracked down Michael McMurtrey.

He had interviewed Dayle's husband before his passing. Michael shared the transcript of that interview. He also had extensive research on the TV program and the aircraft associated with the TV show. Look for his book about the Cessna "Bobcat," to be titled "The Big Book of the Bamboo Bomber" … or something like that.

I found Ron Muerke through a Google search. Ron operates a Sky King memorabilia website. He has the copyright to most television shows. Ron was very helpful in filling in other missing pieces of the story.

That list includes the following people, some of whom were mentioned above:

- "Kip" Grant (Kirby Grant's son)

- Carolyn Grant, Kirby's late wife

- Dayle Fergusson (wife of the late Bill Fergusson, pilot)

- Walter Pierce (Aerobatic pilot with the "Great American Airshow")

- Steve and Amy Brown (Brown Flight School/Sky King Airport)

- Cassie Yde (TVSCO)

- Michael McMurtrey (Author, The Big Book of the Bamboo Bomber)

- Ron Muecke (SkyKing.com)

- David Vanderhoof (the photo of Songbird III at Oshkosh, WI)

- and Paul Erickson who owns a restored Cessna 310-D "Songbird."

I also must thank Wayne Ceynowa and the late Bob Jenkins for their assistance with my research.

I hope you will enjoy the story of the Life and Legend of Kirby "Sky King" Grant. Kirby was a TV hero to a generation or more of pilots and astronauts. They found inspiration in the adventures of the cowboy pilot, who came *Out of the Blue of the Western Sky.*

The Early Years

Kirby Grant's real name was Kirby Grant Hoon, Jr. He was born on November 24th, 1911, in Butte, Montana, and was educated at the University of Washington in Seattle and Whitman College in Walla Walla, Washington.

Kirby was considered a child prodigy. At the young age of 12, he began a professional career as a violinist. He later graduated from the American Conservatory of Music on a scholarship. That was in Chicago, where he majored in violin, voice and drama. It was there in Chicago where he continued his career as a concert violinist, singer and actor.

(Kirby Grant at 12 years old. Source: PBS Television "Back Roads of Montana", episode 23)

In the early days of motion pictures, Chicago was where they made movies. Kirby made his screen debut playing violin in the film "I Dream Too Much" in 1935, which starred Henry Fonda. . Kirby often appeared under the name Robert Stanton in Westerns with George O'Brien before finding a niche as a crooner and orchestra leader in various films from 1941 to 1943.

Kirby also performed on and off throughout his life as a radio and supper club singer and entertainer. Kirby once also dabbled in sculpture.

As Kirby told it, he "didn't go looking for Hollywood." In the late 1930's he had been working as a staff singer for NBC Radio in Chicago when he transferred to California. As an actor, Kirby played leads in low-budget Westerns and other action movies. His movie career was less than spectacular.

Kirby played the part of Canadian Mounties in several movies. Movies like Trail of the Yukon, Call of the Klondike, Northwest Territory, Yukon Gold, and Northern Patrol.

Kirby was the male winner of the Jesse L. Lasky "Gateway to Hollywood" radio talent search in July of 1939. The prize included membership in the Screen Actors Guild. That membership was under the stage name "Robert Stanton". After several years he reverted to his birth name and middle name. The female winner of that year was Dorothy Howe, who became Virginia Vale. If the name doesn't mean anything, you're not old enough. Vale starred in several B-movie Westerns but took various other roles, notably in Blonde Comet (1941), where she played a race car driver.

Kirby's first wife was Barbara Van Brunt. He had dated Barbara for eight years while telling her, "you're too young for me." Kirby and Barbara married in October of 1939. Five years later, right after the war, it seemed that his acting career was beginning to take off. That was when Kirby received what he described as a "Dear John" letter. Barbara had obtained a "quickie divorce" in Mexico. It was the second of at least three marriages for Barbara. Carolyn described it to me this way: "She ran off with Billy Halop, one of the 'Dead-end kids.' " She died in January 1959 In an article in November of 1976, in the Lakeland Ledger said that Kirby returned home broke and divorced "with nowhere to go but up."

Carolyn Gillis was born in her grandmother's home in Brockton, Indiana, and grew up in Terre Haute. She met Kirby when she got a job as a model and a dance teacher working at Wally's Studio in Chicago, making $15 a day.

Chicago was the real hub of the motion picture industry, at that time. The studios often hired models as extras. Carolyn Gillis was one of the extras. She met Kirby on a blind date.

Kirby married Carolyn Jeanne Gillis in 1951 after dating for just ten weeks, . It was a small wedding in the famous "Little Brown Church in the Valley". It was the same place and the year Nancy and Ronald Reagan were married and where Kirby began singing in the choir. As Carolyn related, Kirby's voice was such that everybody stopped singing to listen to Kirby. After a time, the pastor asked Kirby to sing in the church.

Carolyn was born the day Kirby graduated from High School. It was the second marriage for both. Carolyn was married for "three or four years" in her previous marriage. At their marriage, Kirby was thirty-eight, and

Carolyn was twenty-two. She told him she was twenty-three.   That was still ten years younger than his first wife, Barbara. Remember what Kirby had said about Barbara's age?

Most of the following came from cassette recordings that Carolyn Grant sent to me after Kirby's passing.

Kirby had to do a picture at Big Bear the day after the wedding. His producer invited the couple to dinner at the Tail O' The Cock restaurant on their wedding night. Carolyn asked Kirby what she should take to wear, and Kirby said, "blue jeans, or whatever." Carolyn discovered to her dismay, that when people go "out to dinner," it wasn't in "blue jeans or whatever."

Kirby was under contract to do four pictures per year. They were married only a couple of weeks when Kirby had to do two pictures. The films were for Oliver Kirwood's Northwest Mounted Police. Carolyn and Kirby came to call them the "dog" pictures because they featured a big white Chinook dog.

When they got back home, Carolyn's parents drove out to meet her new husband. Her parents had only spoken with Kirby on the phone, so this was the first time they were to meet in person. Carolyn's dad loved to fish, and so did Kirby and Carolyn. Kirby decided to take the group deep sea fishing. They rented a half-day boat and took about fifteen friends and crew from Kirby's live Pacific show.

Kirby worried about the guests getting seasick on the trip. As they were leaving, he passed out Dramamine to the guests but forgot to save some for himself. As the seas got rough and the diesel smell got worse, it was Kirby who became seasick.

The day wasn't a total loss because Carolyn managed to catch a baby shark... that scared her when it wrapped around her leg. On the way back in they threw out the bait. That attracted birds, and Carolyn's mom caught a pelican.

Carolyn told a story about the first time she did Kirby's laundry, and all his shirts came out pink."

They lived in Jackie Coogan's mother's apartment at 106 Pebble Street. Jackie Coogan was a child star. His career began with an appearance in a Charlie Chaplain film classic , *The Kid,* in 1921. He may be better known for playing Uncle Fester in the Adam's Family 1960s TV series. When Kirby found out Carolyn was pregnant, Kirby went up and down the street hollering, "Hey, I'm pregnant." she said that night, and he came home drunk.

The couple had to get a larger apartment, so they moved two doors down from the Coogan apartment. And they bought a boxer dog. .

About to deliver Kendra in August, she told her doctor she didn't want to go to the hospital until she was ready. She wanted to stay with Kirby. The doctor said to her that when the pains were six minutes apart, it was time to go. When the time came they were on the way to the Burbank hospital. Carolyn wanted to stop and get a banana split. Kirby was nervous because he didn't want to be the one to deliver the baby. They stopped anyway at Toluca Lake, near Los Angeles. Kirby brought a Big Ben alarm clock and set it on the counter as the clerk made banana splits for the pair. The clerk didn't charge for the banana splits.

After baby Kendra was born, when Carolyn took her to the doctor for a checkup. Carolyn described how she stopped to see the clerk who had served the banana splits. The clerk said, "I see you made it in time!"

Kirby and his former wife, Barbara, never had a child, so this was his first experience as a father. Kirby wanted to give the new baby its first bath. Carolyn said, "He did a good job. He was a wonderful father."

They made up Kendra's name from a combination of Carolyn's parents' names, Aletha and Kenneth Gillis.

Carolyn was seven months pregnant with their second daughter, Kristin, in 195. Kirby went to work for the Navy. The family moved to Chicago and then to Evanston, Illinois. And the couple bought another boxer dog.

Photo: Kirby, Carolyn and two daughters, Easter, 1956, courtesy of Kip Grant

The youngest child, Kirby Grant, III ("Kip"), was born in 1960. Kip was the couple's only surviving son. Here's why I say that... Steve Brown's father built what became Sky King Airport near Terra Haute, Indiana. He was flying Kirby around the area nearby that airport. When they passed over the Roselawn/Rosemond Cemetery. Kirby said, "I have a son buried there... an infant son." I have not been able to learn the circumstances or the date. There were stories that the couple had married under the stage name "Grant." That was Kirby's middle name and stage name. Son Kip's name appears in public records as Kirby Grant, III. I learned that became an issue for son Kip. He needed a passport to visit Mexico, and his identification didn't all match.

Kirby didn't care much for show business, but he did care about music. There were many famous people in their life. That included Jeanne Cagney, who came to their home "many times." Carolyn later said they have pictures of Jeanne playing the family piano in their home. Jeanne Cagney was James Cagney's sister. She was famous for her performances on stage, in film, radio, and on television from 1939 to 1965.

Carolyn described herself as a bit of an archery enthusiast. When the family lived in Toluca Lake, Kirby set up a target in the backyard. When she accidentally shot one arrow over the fence, William Holden brought it back. As Carolyn said, "I didn't hear anyone say 'ow!' so I guess it was alright."

Carolyn loved entertaining, expecting about twenty to twenty-five people on one occasion. She went to the Toluca Lake market to pick out some "fancy wine." Carolyn said, "you gotta remember, I'm from Terre Haute, Indiana, and if you got Ripple, you were lucky."

Kirby didn't care much for show business, but he did care about music. There were many famous people in their life, including Jeanne Cagney, who came to their home "many times." Carolyn later said they have pictures of Jeanne playing the family piano in their home. Jeanne Cagney was James Cagney's sister and was famous for her performances on stage, in film, radio, and on television from 1939 to 1965.

Carolyn described herself as a bit of an archery enthusiast. When the family lived in Toluca Lake, Kirby set up a target in the backyard. When she accidentally shot one arrow over the fence, William Holden brought it back. As Carolyn said, "I didn't hear anyone say 'ow!' so I guess it was alright."

Carolyn loved entertaining, expecting about twenty to twenty-five people on one occasion. She went to the Toluca Lake market to pick out some "fancy wine." Carolyn said, "you gotta remember, I'm from Terre Haute, Indiana, and if you got Ripple, you were lucky."

(Photo: Carolyn Grant, the artist, courtesy of Kip Grant)

As she was trying to pick out "some fancy wine," a gentleman she described as "dapper-dan" asked, "little lady, are you having a problem picking out your wine?". He was clean-shaven and dressed in a nice gray suit and tie. She explained about the dinner party, and he offered to help. The man made a selection and said, "I think this will go well with your shrimp curry." The gentleman went up to the checkout and said, "if this little lady doesn't like the wine, I want you to put it on my bill."

Carolyn had no idea who it was, so after the gentleman left, she asked the clerk. Later, when she got home and said to Kirby, "Guess who picked out the wine?". Kirby replied, "Gabby Hayes?" It was! Kirby and Gabby Hayes were good friends, but Carolyn had never met him.

Nothing is perfect, and there was a time when Carolyn and Kirby were separated, but then got back together.

The Movies

Kirby's screen debut was playing violin in the movie *Dream Too Much* in 1935. Kirby often appeared under the name Robert Stanton in Westerns with George O'Brien. That was before he found a niche as a crooner and orchestra leader in various films from 1941 to 1943. (Source: Internet Movie Database - IMDB)

Kirby replaced Rod Cameron as the star of Universal's low-budget Westerns. That is according to a story in the New York Times in 1944. The Western roles served as the foundation for his long career. Kirby often lamented being type-cast in those roles.

One part that was not a western was *In Society* with Abbot and Costello, probably their best. Kirby played a cab driver named Peter Evans, around 10 minutes into the movie. That series came to an end in 1949. Universal was reorganized into Universal International. The Abbot and Costello series came to an end. Kirby began appearing in several non-Western roles until 1949. That was when he signed on with Monogram/United Artists to work in Mountie roles until 1954. (Source: www.imdb.com/)

Photo Credit: Library and Archives Canada collectionscan ada.gc.ca

Title	Year	Status	Character
Sweet Adeline	1934		Singing Beer Garden Patron (uncredited)
I Dream Too Much	1935		Violinist (uncredited)
Changing of the Guard	1936	Short	Highlander (uncredited)
In Old Chicago	1937		Mustached Quartette Member - 'Old Virginny' Number (uncredited)
Red River Range	1938		Tex Reilly
Lawless Valley	1938		Ranch Hand (uncredited)
There Goes My Heart	1938		Customer (uncredited)
My Lucky Star	1938		Singing Student on Sleigh Ride (uncredited)
Radio City Revels	1938		Group Singer (uncredited)
Three Sons	1939		Bert Pardway (as Robert Stanton)
Bullet Code	1940		Bud Mathews (as Robert Stanton)
Millionaire Playboy	1940		Bill (uncredited)
The Marines Fly High	1940		Lt. Bob Hobbes (as Robert Stanton)
Mexican Spitfire	1940		Airline Clerk (uncredited)
Always Tomorrow: The Portrait of an American Business	1941		1st Picknicker (uncredited)
Blondie Goes Latin	1941		Hal Trent, Orchestra Leader
My Favorite Blonde	1942		Pilot (uncredited)
Dr. Kildare's Victory	1942		Sgt. Brown (uncredited)
The Power of God	1942		Kenneth Hale
Destination Tokyo	1943		Hornet's Captain (uncredited)
The Stranger from Pecos	1943		Tom Barstow
Bombardier	1943		Pilot (uncredited)
Hello Frisco, Hello	1943		Specialty Singer
Babes on Swing Street	1944		Dick Lorimer
In Society	1944		Peter Evans
Swingtime Holiday	1944	Short	Emcee
Ghost Catchers	1944		Clay Edwards (as Kirby Grant and His Orchestra)

Title	Year	Status	Character
Law Men	1944		Clyde Miller
Rosie the Riveter	1944		Singer at Award Presentation (uncredited)
Sweet Adeline	1934		Singing Beer Garden Patron (uncredited)
I Dream Too Much	1935		Violinist (uncredited)
Changing of the Guard	1936	Short	Highlander (uncredited)
In Old Chicago	1937		Mustached Quartette Member - 'Old Virginny' Number (uncredited)
Red River Range	1938		Tex Reilly
Lawless Valley	1938		Ranch Hand (uncredited)
There Goes My Heart	1938		Customer (uncredited)
My Lucky Star	1938		Singing Student on Sleigh Ride (uncredited)
Radio City Revels	1938		Group Singer (uncredited)
Three Sons	1939		Bert Pardway (as Robert Stanton)
Bullet Code	1940		Bud Mathews (as Robert Stanton)
Millionaire Playboy	1940		Bill (uncredited)
The Marines Fly High	1940		Lt. Bob Hobbes (as Robert Stanton)
Mexican Spitfire	1940		Airline Clerk (uncredited)
Always Tomorrow The Portrait of an American Business	1941		1st Picknicker (uncredited)

Title	Year	Status	Character
Blondie Goes Latin	1941		Hal Trent, Orchestra Leader
My Favorite Blonde	1942		Pilot (uncredited)
Dr. Kildare's Victory	1942		Sgt. Brown (uncredited)
The Power of God	1942		Kenneth Hale
Destination Tokyo	1943		Hornet's Captain (uncredited)
The Stranger from Pecos	1943		Tom Barstow
Bombardier	1943		Pilot (uncredited)
Hello Frisco, Hello	1943		Specialty Singer
Babes on Swing Street	1944		Dick Lorimer
In Society	1944		Peter Evans
Swingtime Holiday	1944	Short	Emcee
Ghost Catchers	1944		Clay Edwards (as Kirby Grant and His Orchestra)
Law Men	1944		Clyde Miller
Rosie the Riveter	1944		Singer at Award Presentation (uncredited)
Hi, Good Lookin'!	1944		King Castle
Chip Off the Old Block	1944		Member - The Jivin' Jacks and Jills (uncredited)
Ditch and Live	1944	Short	Crewman of ditching B-17 (uncredited)
Easy to Look at	1945		Tyler
Penthouse Rhythm	1945		Dick Ryan
Bad Men of the Border	1945		Ted Cameron
Trail to Vengeance	1945		Jeff Gordon
I'll Remember April	1945		Dave Ball

Title	Year	Status	Character
Code of the Lawless	1945		Grant Carter posing as Chad Hilton
Lawless Breed	1946		Ted Everett
Gunman's Code	1946		Jack Douglas aka Duke Masters
Rustler's Round-up	1946		Bob Ryan
She Wrote the Book	1946		Eddie Caldwell
The Spider Woman Strikes Back	1946		Hal Wentley
Blonde Alibi	1946		Henry Rothmore (uncredited)
Gun Town	1946		Kip Lewis
Singin' Spurs	1948		Jeff Carter
Song of Idaho	1948		King Russell
Feudin' Rhythm	1949		Ace Lucky
The Wolf Hunters	1949		RCMP Corporal Rod Webb
Black Midnight	1949		Sheriff Gilbert
Trail of the Yukon	1949		Bob McDonald - Royal NW Mounted
Your Show Time	1949	TV Series	
Call of the Klondike	1950		Corporal Rod Webb
Dial 1119	1950		Reporter (uncredited)
Indian Territory	1950		Lieutenant Randy Mason
Snow Dog	1950		Corporal Rod McDonald - RCMP
Northwest Territory	1951		Corporal Rod Webb
Comin' Round the Mountain	1951		Clark Winfield
Yukon Manhunt	1951		Corporal Rod Webb
Rhythm Inn	1951		Dusty Rhodes
Yukon Gold	1952		RCMP Corporal Rod Webb
Studio One in Hollywood	1952	TV Series	
Cavalcade of America	1953	TV Series	
Northern Patrol	1953		Corporal Rod Webb, RCMP
Family Theatre	1953	TV Series	
Fangs of the Arctic	1953		RCMP Corporal Rod Webb
Yukon Vengeance	1954		Corporal Rod Webb, RCMP
Sky King	1952-1959	TV Series	Sky King / Mason

(Source: www.imdb.com/)

Photo credit: Library and Archives, Candada - Collecti onsCanada.gc.ca

The Sky King TV Series

The role of "Schuyler J. King" was said to have been inspired by a real-life flying policeman. That policeman was Jack Cones, of Twenty Nine Palms in California.

(Source: Autry Museum)

Sky King began as a radio drama. The radio show was first broadcast in 1946. Earl Nightingale played the part of Sky King in that series. It was a fifteen-minute daily radio serial in 1946, and by 1947 it ran twice a week as a 30-minute program. Complete with organ music and sound effects, the Sky King radio show lasted until 1954. Sky King was probably the last of the aviation-based shows on radio. (Superman doesn't count). There were several up to that time. Ask your grandparents if they remember Speed Gibson or Tailspin Tommy. Then there was Anne of the Airlines, Captain Midnight and Hop Harrigan. Others included Howie Wing, Air Stories of the World War, and the Air Adventures of Jimmy Allen.

Trivia question: Who was the announcer on the radio show? It was the late Mike Wallace, best known for his role on 60 Minutes on CBS. Wallace once said that the Sky King announcing job began his broadcasting career.

In the radio version, Sky King flew two airplanes. One was a propeller aircraft, dubbed "Songbird." The other was a jet they called "Flying Arrow".." In the radio show, no particular models were identified. Still, in one episode, "The Lady Sheriff," the "flying Arrow" jet carried two passengers. In the script, the Sky King character claimed that it was equipped with a "20-millimeter cannon".

The "Flying Arrow" was said to have played a cameo role in a later TV episode. That episode used involving stock footage of a Bell P-59A Airacomet. The P-59A was the USAF's first jet fighter, but that rumor does not line up with the list of known shows. It was a single-seat twin jet-engine fighter. The plane, designed and built by Bell Aircraft for use in the first World War. We will have More about the Sky King aircraft in the next chapter.

Sky King Television Productions

In 1954 Kirby was already beginning his role as Sky King while playing Canadian Mountie roles. The Television role had grown out of the earlier radio series. There were 72 Sky King television shows produced from 1951 to 1958. The show lived on in reruns into the 1960s; and was again syndicated some years later.

It is well known that there were and are only 72 shows produced. There are stories about 130 original shows. That number would include some were "lost" in a fire at Bonded Film Storage in New York. Those stories are not true. However, that being said, when I counted the titles, the total comes to 73. First season: 20, second season: 20, third season 20 shows, and the fourth season: 13 shows. 60 plus 13 is 73. (See the list later in this chapter).

(Photo source: Imagezone.com)

According to one source, much of the series was shot at Corriganville, a stage set owned by "Crash" Corrigan. (Source: AeroMovies.FR)

The series was a low-cost, black and white production, with a large part of the budget going to operating the planes. "Sky King" was first broadcast on NBC, then it moved to ABC, and finally to CBS Saturday mornings. The production schedule most often involved shooting two shows each week.

The Sky King show was produced at three separate times as the sponsors changed. In 1951 and 1952, the sponsor was Derby Foods, advertising Peter Pan Peanut Butter. Back then, Derby Foods was a subsidiary of Swift and Company. Peter Pan, by the way, was the first peanut butter sold in plastic jars. The brand is now part of Con-Agra. Between 1955-1956 and 1957-1958 were sponsored by Nabisco. That is the sponsor most associated with the show. The sponsor was identified by an animated stick figure cowboy and horse. Nabisco syndicated (distributed) to locations where products were not producing adequate sales. The Sky King show succeeded in boosting sales in those markets.

Revolvy.com reports the television show first appeared on Sunday afternoons on NBC-TV. That was between September 16, 1951, and October 26, 1952. The following year, those episodes were replayed on ABC's Saturday morning lineup. In September 21, 1953 it made its prime-time debut on ABC's Monday night lineup. In Cessna's hometown of Wichita, Kansas, it was broadcast at 6 pm. The show ran twice-a-week in August and September of 1954, before ABC canceled it.

More episodes were produced when the fourth season of the show went into syndication in 1955. The series aired well into the sixties and beyond.

The last new episode, "Mickey's Birthday", aired on March 8, 1959. In the shows, "Mickey" was a relative of Sky King, portrayed in three 1959 episodes by child actor Gary Hunley. (Source: IMDB)

The Sky King TV series resurfaced on the CBS Saturday schedule in reruns until September, 1966. I remember seeing the show in Central Florida on WDBO-TV, Channel 6, CBS. when the program director was Walter "Uncle Walt" Sickles.

Nabisco either sold or gave the series and the rights to Kirby Grant in 1959. In the 1970s Bob Yde (Television Syndication Company) syndicated the series. In my late teens I had a job as a film editor at television stations in the Tampa area. I became involved with the cleaning and shipping of the television prints for TVSCO. We set up shop in a spare bedroom of our small home near Sanford, Florida. Michael McMurtrey conducted interviews and research about the television show for his book. Mike told me the video rights to the television shows later went to "a gentleman in Tennessee". That "gentleman" is Bill Campbell. Now the rights for all but four are now owned by Ron Muercke, who operates the SkyKing.com website . The last four episodes of season 4 are currently in the Public Domain.

Most of the action takes place in the "cowboy country" of Arizona. The external scenes were actually shot in the desert of southern California. The Flying Crown Ranch was really a house in the Apple Valley subdivision. The home is near the small airport of the same name. The cast stayed at the Apple Valley Inn, owned by Roy Rogers and Dale Evans at the time. Several scenes were shot in the vicinity in the mountains of San Bernardino, near China Lake and George AFB military base.

The show was a success. Sky King became "the favorite flying cowboy," as it said in the credits and the commercials airing within the show. In recent years, the Sky King shows have become somewhat of a cult series. As was typical of children's shows of the time, rarely were any shots fired and nobody was ever killed in the action.

Gloria Winters played the role of Penny King, niece to "Uncle Sky" in episodes from 1952 to 1959. In an interview, Gloria claimed that she was a licensed pilot. She met her husband on the set of the Sky King series when he was the "sound man". In a television interview, Gloria said that her husband was also a licensed pilot.

In Jimmy Buffet's song, Pencil Thin Mustache, includes a reference to Penny King's character in the Sky King show. It's in the third verse:

> I remember bein' buck-toothed and skinny
> Writin' fan letters to Sky's niece Penny
> Oh I wish I had a pencil-thin mustache
> Then I could solve some mysteries, too

One responder to our online survey told us "To this day I still have a crush on Sky's Niece Penny."

Many male viewers found a similar attraction to "Penny". The character never actually had a boyfriend in the series. In the shows, her attention was to flying and horses. Gloria herself had a running romance with horses since the age of two. Her real family lived on Rodeo Drive in Beverly Hills. A bridle path ran down the center of the street, where several movie and Western stars exercised their horses. Gloria wanted to be a cowgirl. In the Sky King show, she got her wish.

In one episode, "her" horse was a small black-and-white pinto. The scripts sometimes called for her to ride other horses. Gloria, was all of five feet, one and a half inches. It's understandable why she preferred "short" horses. "When I have to mount a tall horse it becomes a real production".

Gloria was introduced to a trick horse known as "Tony". Tony was the "Wonder Horse". She never trained a horse to do tricks. Gloria was impressed with "Tony". He could come at a whistle, walk on his hind legs, do the "prayer" trick, play sick, nod his head in answer to questions, and whinny on cue. Gloria couldn't get the horse to do any of those things until the trainer showed her how, and then it was easy. She could motion with a whip and say "up" and Tony would respond by rising up on his hind legs. (Source, another obscure un-credited magazine reprint)

Gloria Winters died on Aug. 14, 2010 at her home in Vista, Calif., north of San Diego. She was in her late 70s. Her family told the Los Angeles

Times the cause of death was complications of pneumonia. (Source: New York Times, Anita Gates)

Ronald F. Hagerthy was born March 9, 1932. He appeared as "Skipper" in 19 Sky King episodes along with a long list of drama and sit-com rolls. During the time the Sky King series was in production, Haggerthy was drafted into the army. The Sky King script kept saying that he was in the Air Force, hoping he could one day return to the series. It didn't happen. After his release from the Army Hagerthy did get. At last check, Ron was living in California. He would would be 91 in 2023. .

Ewing Mitchell played Grover County Sheriff Mitch in the series. He played similar roles with Gene Autry (14) and Roy Rogers (4 shows). He also appeared in one episode of the CBS series The Millionaire and a long list of other drama and western shows. He acted in the first season of The Adventures of Rin Tin Tin . Mitchell, like Kirby Grant, also had a musical background. Mitchell passed away in 1988 in La Jolla, California. His death was reportedly from a stroke resulting from a fall from a ladder.

Composer Herschel Burke Gilbert composed most of the musical score. At least, that is according to a Wikipedia post.

There was even one Sky King script that involved a space shot. A well-understood rule on the set was that there was to be no smoking in front of the kids. Remember, this was back in the 1950s.

On August 28, 1995, the Family Channel decided to rerun the series. Gus Lucas, Family Channel VP of Programming described it as "corny to the point of being hilarious". Critics were more kind during the show's original run. They described the writing of the series as "above average", but "not so much" for the acting. Some of the actors who appeared in the series were Jill St. John and Glenn Strange. Darryl Hickman (better known for his roles in Doby Gillis and Gilligan) also appeared in the series. Sammee Tong played a part in one show. None of the stars of the television show received any royalties on airplay.

A 1985 report in the Sun Sentinel newspaper said

"Mr. Grant tried repeatedly but unsuccessfully for several years to revive the television series that made him famous. He dreamed of shooting a new Sky King series in Florida and often spoke enthusiastically of using Kennedy Space Center and Embry-Riddle Aeronautical University in Daytona Beach as story locations."

The Accidental Stunt Pilot

In her blog, Dayle Fergusson relates how her husband, Bill, became involved with the Sky King show. Back then, in the late Fifties, Bill was working for Cessna Aircraft Company in Wichita, Kansas. He was national sales manager for their new twin, the Cessna 310. Bill flew around the country, demonstrating the plane to potential customers. The sponsor of the show, Nabisco, approached Cessna about providing a new plane for the series. They had retired the old Cessna T-50 (the Bamboo Bomber). Cessna jumped at the idea as a great way to promote their new twin airplane. They agreed to provide the airplane at no cost for several weeks of filming.

(Photo: the three Fergussons and the Songbird III promotion plane)

Pilot Bill Fergusson didn't plan on piloting the new Songbird for the TV production.

*Bill Fergusson and the Songbird II, Photo provided courtesy
of Dayle Furguson*

Here is what I learned from Dayle Fergusson.... Bill delivered a sparkling new Cessna 310B to the filming site at Apple Valley, California. The stunt pilot next on the assignment list for the job was only a single-engine rated pilot. Cessna told Bill to stay long enough to check out the new guy for a twin-engine rating, and then return to Wichita. "He's doing great," Bill reported to his boss, Frank Martin, "but I can't sign him off. The insurance company would never approve it." "What do you mean?" his boss exploded. "The flying involves landing on roads and dry lake beds, flying under bridges, and landing with both engines shut down. He's just not up to that sort of flying yet. Maybe they can provide another pilot.", Bill explained. The McGowan Brothers were already breathing down Martin's neck, anxious to begin filming. Everyone's blood pressure was rising. Martin snapped: "Well you stay and do the flying yourself," and he slammed down the phone. Bill soon discovered it was some of the most fun flying he had ever done since his military days.

For the next two weeks, his job was to play double for Sky King. He wore a big cowboy hat for close-up shots at the controls of the plane. He put the plane through an intensive program of adventurous flying. The production company created a library of every imaginable sequence they might need. Months later they added more sequences using a different plane to add to the library. There's a quote in Wikipedia referencing a published article "310B Goes to Hollywood". It quotes Bill Ferguson as recalling how Kirby Grant "flew the 310B like a real pro in no time". I finally found the article as a scan from an old website. It appears to have been written around between 1956 and 1959, which would have been episodes 40 to 73. That was the time the 310 began appearing in the Sky King shows. The article's author's name does not appear in the reprint. It's just as well it doesn't. The quote from Bill Ferguson does not actually appear in the article. The quote also completely contradicts statements in an interview Bill had with Michael McMurtrey in later years.

The TV series, was made for the kids or the housewives of middle America of the fifties. Kirby voiced ads for Peter Pan peanut butter or Nabisco biscuits. His suave voice in the ads was in the purest traditions of the singing cowboys of the time, including Roy Rogers and Gene Autry. Kirby Grant was as much a true singer as any of the "singing cowboys," but he never sang in the TV series. Speaking of singing cowboys, Kirby, Gene Autry and Roy Rogers were all friends. Many of the episodes start with the same sentence: "Out of the blue of the western sky, comes Sky King!" But in some, the announcer says "Out of the CLEAR blue..." You can hear several examples of the opening sequence on YouTube.   One is found here:

(Scan with mobile device)

and the other is found here:

(Scan with mobile device)

So the answer to which one was "real" is... both. If you know anybody of the right age you might win a free beer with that trivia question. Some references list a third variation, "FROM out of the blue..."

Meanwhile, back at the ranch...

In the television shows, the exterior of a home in a subdivision near what was once the Apple Valley Airport was the Flying Crown Ranch. It has been (understandably) remodeled extensively since the time of the television show.

(www.thisdayinaviation.com - Jack Chertoff Television Productions)

This still image captured from the series shows the Songbird parked at the "Flying Crown Ranch". The show made it appear that it was at the front door of a large ranch estate. In some cases the they taxied the plane down streets from the nearby airport. The house in the residential area used for the exterior shots. The airport that appeared in most of the TV shows was not in Arizona. It was the Apple Valley Airport, in Apple Valley, CA. To find the location, enter the coordinates in Google Earth or find it on an aeronautical map: 34°31'14.99"N, 117°13'19.46"W. Nearby, the Apple Valley Inn served as the base of operations. Today there is a Super Target shopping center where the airport had been. What remains today is a small piece of the original run-up area. It appears southwest of the intersection of Dale Evans Parkway and Thunderbird Road near California Highway 18. It appears in this aerial view.

(Image credit: Google Earth)

Another example of a Sky King myth is found in a newspaper item dated June 11, 2006. The title is "Sky King star landed in Valley Center". In it, reporter Vincent Nicolas Rossi, says:

"In real life, Kirby Grant, the actor who played Sky King, was indeed a flier and a rancher, and until his death in 1985, his ranch was in Valley Center. Just south of the intersection of Lake Wohlford Road and Valley Center Road is the remnant of an airstrip. This was Grant's private strip, according to Bob Lerner of the Valley Center History Museum. Grant's home was at the end of the airstrip, fronting on Valley Center Road. "

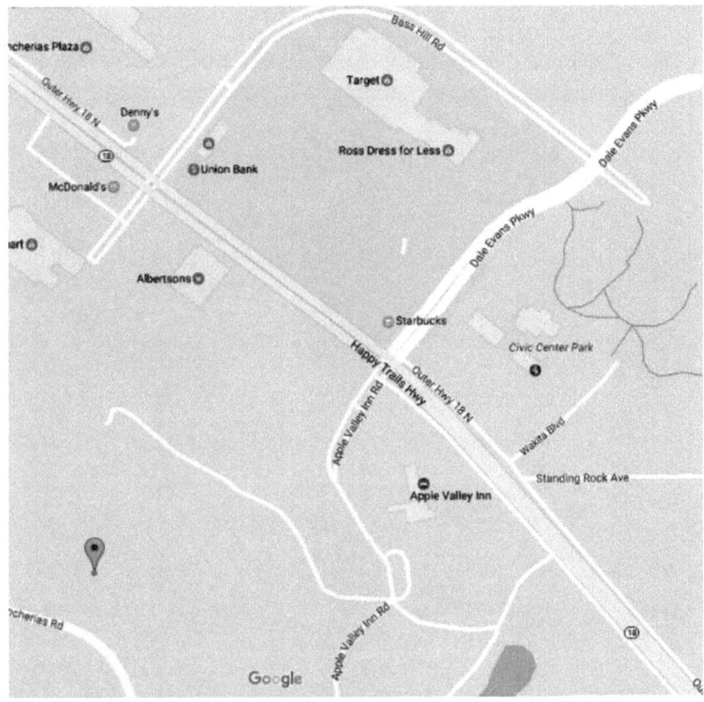

(Image credit: Google Earth) Location map today

We won't go into detail to point them out, but there are more than a few problems with the story.

The Shows

Directors:

Hollingsworth MORSE (15 episodes, 1952), Jodie COPELAN (12 episodes, 1956-1958), Stuart E. McGOWAN (12 episodes, 1956-1958), Clark L. PAYLOW (11 episodes, 1956-1959), Paul LANDRES Oliver DRAKE (2 episodes, 1958), Richard C. KAHN (2 episodes, 1958), William WITNEY (4 episodes, 1959), William J. HOLE Jr. (2 episodes, 1958-1959), and Herbert L. STROCK (2 episodes, 1958).

Main actors:

Kirby Grant (Sky King) (*72 episodes,1952-1959), Gloria Winters (Penny King (*72 episodes,1952-1959), Ewing Mitchell (Sheriff Mitch Hargrove) (26 episodes,1955-1959), Ron Hagerthy (Clipper King) (19 episodes,1952-1955), Norman OLLESTAD (Bob Carey) (10 episodes,1956-1957), Bill Hale (Bert) (6 episodes, 1956-1959), Dennis Moore (Charlie) (5 episodes,1956-1959), Rusty Wescoatt (Frisco) (5 episodes,1956-1959), Monte Blue (Sheriff Hollister) (5 episodes,1952-1955).

*We have titles for 73 episodes listed below.

Music:

Eve Newman, music editor for Death Valley Days and 8 episodes of Sky King

Alec Compinsky- Music Supervisor for 22 Sky King episodes, also The Third Man, Death Valley Days (25) , Broken Arrow, Pony Express, Crossroads, Jungle Jim (1) and uncredited in An American in Paris, not to forget 20 episodes of Bozo The World's Most Famous Clown, in 1958.

Photography:

Carl Berger, Robert Pittack, William Bradford, Hal McAlpin, Brydon Baker, and Mack Stengler.

Producers:

Clark L. Paylow, Jack Chertok

Production Company:

Jack Chertok Television Productions, McGowan Productions The shows were produced in black and white, at around $30,000 per episode. That was a relatively low cost for the time. Although the action in the shows takes place in Arizona, the external scenes were shot in the desert of southern California. Several scenes were also shot in the vicinity of the San Bernardino mountains near China Lake and George Air Force Base. In all, four seasons of Sky King were produced. The shows ran from 22 to 24 minutes in length. The initial production ran from 1951 to 1952, produced by Jack Chertok.

Jack Chertok produced a number of shorts and documentaries. That was before he was hired to produce the first 19 Sky King shows in 1951. Chertok went on to produce The Legend of the Lone Ranger movie in 1952, the Lone Ranger Rides Again movie in 1955. Between those years, he produced 182 episodes of the Lone Ranger TV series between 1949 and 1955. He also produced other long-forgotten TV shows. The list includes Cavalcade of America, Private Secretary and My Living Doll. He later produced 109 episodes of My Favorite Martian, from 1963 to 1966. He was executive producer of a TV movie, The Iron Men, in 1966. Born in Atlanta in July of 1906, Chertok died in Los Angeles in 1995 at the age of 88.

Production of the Sky King series returned in 1955 with producers Stuart and Darrell McGowan with a different T-50 airplane, repainted to display the N number of the original aircraft for ground sequences, mixed with stock footage of the plane used in the first series. The show had a new sponsor when Nabisco acquired the rights to the franchise. The series appeared on the NBC, ABC and CBS networks. It was later shown in syndication to individual stations. Even today, it lives on as a cult favorite on YouTube and bootleg DVDs.

There is a story about a fire at Bonded Film Storage on Ninth Avenue in New York causing destruction of many of the Sky King master prints. The facts dispute that story. My contact, with Amanda at the New York Fire Department Museum historian, failed to find any data for a fire at that address. Ron Muecke currently owns the copyrights to most of the shows. Ron says there are no "lost episodes". He was able to obtain all but eight of the masters from the person Kirby Grant sold them to. The shows can be widely viewed on YouTube and elsewhere online or even purchased online. However, the only legal copies are DVDs that have been digitally re-mastered from the original film prints. Those that are found at Muecke's website, SkyKing.com.

The author acquired five of the film prints that were distributed to television stations. They had been reported lost by the shipper, Railway Express. Then some years later, they somehow turned up and were delivered to my door. Now after decades of storage under the wrong conditions, the acetate films are crumbling and useless. Actually, I only have four. Kirby Grant asked for one to take to an event in his honor at the Smithsonian sometime around 1980. They were still usable then. I assume that's where my fifth copy remains. More on that in a later chapter.

Sky King shows:

Season 1 (20 shows) - Songbird I (Cessna AT-50)

S1, Ep1 - 5 Apr. 1952
    Operation Urgent
    During a fierce thunderstorm, Sky picks up a mayday call from a Air Force courier plane which is about to run out of gas. The Air Force requests Sky's assistance in locating the downed aircraft because the pilot is transporting secret documents that are of interest to foreign governments. Sky locates the plane wreck, but the pilot is nowhere to be found. When he discovers that the navigational instruments have been tampered with, Sky fears that enemy agents may have located and stolen the secret plans and are headed for the nearby Mexican border.

    S1, Ep2 - 19 Apr. 1952
    Carrier Pigeon
    When Penny discovers a wounded carrier pigeon carrying a valuable ruby attached to its leg, Sky suspects a gang of jewel smugglers is operating

in the area. With the help of a Mexican police detective, Sky sets up to break up the criminal operation.

S1, Ep3 - 3 May 1952
Stage Coach Robbers
A crooked express agent fakes a hold-up to steal gold from his company's vault. He uses an old stagecoach to get the stolen loot out of town.

S1, Ep4 - 17 May 1952
Deadly Cargo
While helping a friend run his freight airline after an accident, Sky stumbles across a gold-smuggling operation.

S1, Ep5 - 31 May 1952
Jim Bell's Triumph
Sky's efforts to prove corruption in the county clerk's office nearly result in disaster, when Sky's foreman, a non-pilot, must land the Songbird when Clipper becomes too ill to fly the plane.

S1, Ep6 - 14 Jun. 1952
Designing Woman
Sky becomes suspicious when a Eastern woman shows up in Grover claiming to be the long-lost niece and heir of a dead rancher.

S1, Ep7 - 28 Jun. 1952
One for the Money
Penny picks up the wrong suitcase at the airport and discovers it's full of counterfeit money. Sky suspects that a young former engraver might be involved.

S1, Ep8 - 12 Jul. 1952
Danger Point
A rancher disinherits his nephew in favor of his young son. When the rancher is murdered the young man is blamed. Sky hopes that by faking a jailbreak, the real murderer will be forced into the open, but the plan backfires when Clipper and the young man are kidnapped.

S1, Ep9 - 26 Jul. 1952
Desperate Character
Sky King picks up a young hitchhiker who refuses to divulge his identity, or where he's been or where he's going. Determined to fill in the blank spaces on the young man's resume, Sky learns that he is an escapee from a boy's reformatory who was involved in a recent bank robbery.

S1, Ep10 - 9 Aug. 1952
The Man Who Forgot
A young rancher disappears after the man attempting to foreclose on his mortgage is murdered. Sky is convinced that the man is innocent and that there's another explanation for the man's apparent flight.

S1, Ep11 - 23 Aug. 1952
The Threatening Bomb
Eastern gangsters set up a protection racket near Grover and the local ranchers appeal to Sky for help.

S1, Ep12 - 6 Sep. 1952
Speak No Evil
The drug Sky delivers to a critically ill man does more than save his life; the medicine causes the man to confess that he's a former criminal who has attempted to go straight.

S1, Ep13 - 20 Sep. 1952
Two-Gun Penny
Angry that Sky and Clipper won't allow her to join the search for a missing refugee professor, Penny slaps on a pair of six-shooters and launches her own investigation.

S1, Ep14 - 4 Oct. 1952
Formula for Fear
Penny sees a man escape from a doctor's office, and is informed that the man is a dangerous mental patient. Sky looks into the incident, and soon finds himself mixed up in foreign spies and poison gas.

S1, Ep15 - 18 Oct. 1952
The Giant Eagle
Sky investigates a series of mysterious payroll robberies, where the police chase the robbers only to see their getaway car mysteriously disappear.

S1, Ep16 - 8 Nov. 1952
Blackmail
A local banker is blackmailed by two former confederates who aware of a crime he committed over twenty years ago and was never apprehended.

S1, Ep17 - 22 Nov. 1952
Wings of Justice
A couple of Easterners claim to have traveled west to visit a dude ranch, but are actually a pair of con artists willing to commit murder to obtain a ranch with a rich uranium deposit on it.

S1, Ep18 - 6 Dec. 1952
Destruction from the Sky
Sky teams up with a military intelligence officer to track down a foreign agent who blew up a secret government project.

S1, Ep19 - 20 Dec. 1952
The Porcelain Lion
Sky stumbles across a dead pilot and suspicious looking plane wreck and discovers that the man was murdered and the crash never happened. He

learns that the plane was carrying a number of valuable pieces of ancient Chinese art, all of which are missing from the plane's cargo hold.

Season 2 (20 shows) - Songbird I (Cessna AT-50) sponsored by Nabisco.

S2, Ep1 - 2 Jan. 1956
The Neckerchief
Sky attempts to help a young man recently paroled from prison get started again, but the ex-convict's former friends frame him for a bank robbery.

S2, Ep2 - 2 Jan. 1956
Manhunt
Sky King joins the hunt for two escaped convicts and their hostage, the local banker's son.

S2, Ep3 - 9 Jan. 1956
The Plastic Ghost
A distress signal from a ghost town leads Sky and Penny to a dangerous criminal and his hostage.

S2, Ep4 - 9 Jan. 1956
The Rainbird
Village Indians give their medicine man two days to bring an end to a drought. Sky helps out.

S2, Ep5 - 30 Jan. 1956
The Crystal Trap
While the towns people wait for the unveiling of a uranium map, the map is stolen. Sky King comes to the rescue.

S2, Ep6 - 30 Jan. 1956
The Red Tentacle

When several local Chinese residents are beaten and refuse to tell why, Sky intervenes.

S2, Ep7 - 6 Feb. 1956
Boomerang
Sky King and Penny turn the tables on foreign agents conspiring to blackmail an important refugee scientist.

S2, Ep8 - 27 Feb. 1956
The Geiger Detective
Some bandits steal a payroll and escape into the hills. They hold a Uranium prospector captive. Sky uses a Geiger counter to help track down the robbers.

S2, Ep9 - 27 Feb. 1956
Golden Burro
Penny finds a prospector dying in the desert beside burrows carrying gold ore.

S2, Ep10 - 5 Mar. 1956
Rustlers on Wheels
A young rancher has 60 head of cattle stolen. Sky discovers the cattle were taken away in trucks with diamond-shape tire tread.

S2, Ep11 - 5 Mar. 1956
The Silver Grave
A long-forgotten train robber and a phony historian lead Sky King into a mystery.

S2, Ep12
12 Mar. 1956
Uninvited Death
Sky and Penny unwittingly become involved in sabotage when they visit their friends Major Dave and Denise McKay. An enemy agent has attached a time bomb to Major McKay's car, setting the fuse to explode while the Major is working at an army special-projects base. When Denise and Penny borrow the Major's car, they are placed in grave peril.

S2, Ep13 -19 Mar. 1956
Fish Out of Water
An escape convict sets out to kill the judge who sentenced him. Sky and the judge are on a fishing trip and Penny has to warn them.

S2, Ep14 - 26 Mar. 1956
Diamonds on a Sky-Hook
Sky King devises a sky hook so he can pick up diamonds from an airplane.

S2, Ep15 - 2 Apr. 1956
Flood of Fury
During a major flood, Sky, Penny and Bob assist the authorities in their rescue efforts. Unfortunately, three of the men they rescue are murderous escaped felons who force their rescuers to help them rob a flooded bank.

S2, Ep16 - 2 Apr. 1956
Rocket Story
Sky hosts two government agents at the Flying Crown Ranch the night before a secret rocket test, but one of the men is an imposter.

S2, Ep17 - 23 Apr. 1956
Rodeo Round-Up
During the El Dorado Rodeo two men rob the safe of the $10,000.00 that was gathered for the hospital fund.

S2, Ep18 - 23 Apr. 1956
Showdown
Penny and Bob Carey set out on horseback to track down thieves who have stolen four of Sky King's horses. Bob is hurt and Sky arranges a showdown.

S2, Ep19 - 23 Apr. 1956
Land o' Cotton
Sky king rescues a Mexican family who are trapped into working for an unscrupulous cotton farmer.

S2, Ep20 - 30 Apr. 1956
Dust of Destruction
After a young rancher inherits his uncle's farm and tries to raise alfalfa to pay off a debt, Sky King has to solve the mystery of why it was poisoned.

Season 3 (20 shows) - Songbird II (Cessna 310B)

S3, Ep1 - 29 Dec. 1957
Mystery Horse
Sky is forced to take drastic action to save the life of a famous racehorse trapped in a canyon.

S3, Ep2 - 29 Dec. 1957
Double Trouble
When a man who looks like Sky King steals the Songbird and attempts to blow up a Navy missile center, Sky borrows a jet to chase him.

S3, Ep3 - 5 Jan. 1958
Note for a Dam
Rancher Angus McGonicle keeps finding strange bottles with lit wicks and notes, floating down the river, threatening the dam, which King traces to a psychotic old hermit upstream. There, he traps King and Penny, then sets out to dynamite the dam in a rowboat.

S3, Ep4 - 5 Jan. 1958
Bad Actor
Sky and Penny discover a movie set on location. They watch a real robbery thinking that it had been staged, and then Sky finds the robber who had been working with the crew.

S3, Ep5 - 12 Jan. 1958
Fight for Oil

An old friend of Sky's asks for help after someone attempts to kill him because of his oil well.

S3, Ep6 - 12 Jan. 1958
Lost Boy
Sky King and the Songbird are asked to help search for a boy whose life is in danger.

S3, Ep7 -26 Jan. 1958
The Brain and the Brawn
While investigating crime at the County Fair, Sky and Penny encounter a sinister hypnotist.

S3, Ep8 - 26 Jan. 1958
The Feathered Serpent
After Penny finds a homing pigeon with an emerald attached to its leg, she alerts Sky and they follow to see where it goes.

S3, Ep9 - 22 Feb. 1958
The Circus Clown Mystery
When a police bulletin describes a thief as over seven feet tall, Sky and Penny head to the circus to find him.

S3, Ep10 - 22 Feb. 1958
Dead Man's Will
When a man claims that the land on which the clinic for poverty-stricken Indians is built belongs to him, Sky steps in to prove he's wrong.

S3, Ep11 - 11 Mar. 1958
Cindy, Come Home
When the doctor tells Sky that the only thing that will save a little girl is the return of her father, Sky sets out to find him.

S3, Ep12 - 9 Mar. 1958
Rodeo Decathlon
When a young man is injured in the rodeo, Sky helps out by transporting him to the hospital and participating in the events

S3, Ep13 - 9 Mar. 1958
Abracadabra
Sky and Penny attend a Hollywood party and meet a magician. The fun ceases when a precious diamond is reported missing.

S3, Ep14 - 9 Mar. 1958
Triple Exposure
Sky and Penny try to recover a valuable stamp collection with the help of a newspaper photographer.

S3, Ep15 - 16 Mar. 1958
The Haunted Castle
Sky and Penny are asked to investigate stories about a strange house. It had been said that it was "haunted".

S3, Ep16 - 16 Mar. 1958
Man Hunt
Fearing he has killed another boy, Joe Belden, recently released from reform school, flees into the desert. Sheriff Hargrove knows that the Joe's opponent survived the fight, but also knows that Joe, now heavily armed, will think that the law officers are intent on arresting him. He calls upon Sky, whom Joe trusts, to join the man-hunt.

S3, Ep17 - 16 Mar. 1958
Danger at the Sawmill
After almost being run down by a lumber truck, Sky and Penny investigate and learn that the local timber workers are being victimized.

S3, Ep18 - 23 Mar. 1958
Sleight of Hand
Sky and his friend Davey Wilson fall into a trap set for them by crooked gamblers.

S3, Ep19 - 23 Mar. 1958
The Runaway

Sky and Penny search for their friend, Davey, who ran away to the mountains after being pursued by gunmen.

S3, Ep20 - 30 Mar. 1958
Stop That Train
Penny is captured by three men who plan to dynamite the train. Sky and Davey race (or rather fly) to the rescue.
Season 4 (13 shows) Songbird II (Cessna 310B)

S4, Ep1 - 28 Dec. 1958
The Wild Man
Sky and Penny try to clear a gentle, animal-loving "wildman" who has been blamed for the robbery of a logging company payroll.

S4, Ep2 - 28 Dec. 1958
Sky Robbers
Sky and Penny enter an air race, and it's soon discovered that the main office has been robbed and all of the receipts have been stolen. Sky suspects that one of the contestants in the race is the culprit and is using the race to make his getaway.

S4, Ep3 - 28 Dec. 1958
A Dog Named Barney
Sky follows the seeing-eye dog of a blind newsboy, who he believes will lead him to a holdup man living with a party of wolf hunters.

S4, Ep4 - 28 Dec. 1958
Bullet Bait
Sky is holding a wedding at the Flying Crown Ranch. The ceremony is interrupted, however, when two gangsters kidnap the groom and threaten his fiancé.

S4, Ep5 - 4 Jan. 1959
Money Has Wings
Four pilots for Wellman Air Freight Lines are injured in the first month of a contract for the company to carry s large payroll. In order to find out what's going on, Sky goes undercover as a security guard.

S4, Ep6 - 4 Jan. 1959
Frog Man
Young Jimmy Ness has recently come into, and started spending, lots of money. He won't tell his aunt where he is getting the money from, and his dad is away working at the Flying Crown Ranch. Hoodlums find out about Jimmy's money.

S4, Ep7 - 1 Feb. 1959
Terror Cruise
While Sky is training with his naval reserve unit, Penny visits friends who cruise Central America on their large sailboat. When three escaped prisoners commandeer their vessel, it's up to Sky and the U.S. Navy to rescue his niece and her friends.

S4, Ep8 - 1 Feb. 1959
Operation Urgent aka Runaway Truck
Sky learns that a t neighbor, driving a truck full of children back from a picnic has accidentally taken an overdose of sleeping pills.

S4, Ep9 - 1 Feb. 1959
Bounty Hunters
When marauding coyotes begin to kill his calves, Sky hires two flying bounty hunters to kill the animals. When more dead calves are found, Sky discovers that the men he has hired are using his ranch to smuggle jewels, not kill vermin.

S4, Ep10 - 1 Mar. 1959 (PD)
Dead Giveaway
Sky's visitor Mickey goes exploring on his new pony and is captured by thieves guarding a large supply of stolen cars.

S4, Ep11 - 22 Feb. 1959 (PD)
A Mickey for Sky
Young Mickey, a distant relative of Sky's, is traveling to visit the Flying Crown Ranch while his guardian is out of the country. En route, he

overhears two men discuss shooting a foreign visitor and is determined to warn the man of his peril.

S4, Ep12 -1 Mar. 1959 ((PD)
Ring of Fire
Sky tries to help an old Indian chief who is very sick, but he won't go to the hospital for treatment because he would rather die on his own tribe's land.

S4, Ep13 - 8 Mar. 1959 (PD)
Mickey's Birthday
While visiting an amusement park on his birthday, Mickey wins a model airplane at a shooting gallery. Unfortunately, two smugglers have hidden a valuable pearl in the airplane and will stop at nothing to get it back. [1]
(PD indicates Public Domain)

---

1. (Source: www.imdb.com/title/tt0043232/)

The Aircraft

When they were not flying around, Sky King and Penny spend a lot of time in their station wagon (a 1951 Plymouth Woody Station wagon. Later there was a 1955 Chrysler New Yorker, and finally a 1959 Buick Invicta. In the air, they fly mostly Cessna planes. In the course of the television production, there were two Cessna models of the famous "Songbird" aircraft: the T-50/AT-17 and the 310. However, a number of other aircraft also made appearances in the series.

Series 1:
- -Cessna T-50 Bobcat, s/n 6117, s / n 43-32179, NC67832

- -Cessna UC-78B Bobcat s/n 6402, s / n 43-32464, N68311

- -Cessna T-50 Bobcat, s/n 3305, N4571N

- -Cessna T-50 Bobcat, s/n 450, N53378

Series 2,3,4
- -Cessna 310B s/n 35548, N5348A

- -Cessna 310B s/n 35735, N6635B

- -Cessna 310D, s/n 3911, N6817T

- -Cessna 170 s/n 18188, NC2678V ("Skipper")

- -North American NA-145 Navion s/n NAV-4-22, N91132

- -Lockheed 12A Junior s/n c / n 1243, N60775

- -Culver Dart G ("Penny")

- -Beech D18S s/n A-136, N44647

- -Beech 35 Bonanza s/n D765, N3306V

- -Grumman F9F-6 Cougar, Modex "105" BuNo. 128158

- -Aeronca L-16A s/n 7EC503, N7454B

- -Douglas C-47B s/n 25768, s / n 43-48507, N91014

- -Bell 47 (on the ground)

Another Cessna 310B (s/n 35735) that appeared in the series was built in 1958. Little is known about this plane other than it was likely destroyed on landing September 17, 1969, in Denton, Tx, after a trip from Ardmore, OK. According to some reports, it belonged to Viking Aero Service at the time. An accident matching the description appears in the NTSB reports. The N Number was later reassigned to a Beach aircraft.

At the start of the war, Cessna obtained contracts to build the AT-17 Bobcat version of the aircraft for both Canada and the United States. According to Wikipedia, the AT-17 had a top speed of 195 mph, a cruise speed of 175 mph, and was used during World War II to fill the gap between single-engine trainers and twin-engine combat aircraft.

Cessna T-50/AT-17

Various versions of the Cessna T-50, known as the "Bamboo Bomber", were used by the military and after the war there were a lot of them around. In the first 38 episodes of the original Nabisco production in the 1950s, the plane was a World War II surplus UC-78B, owned by legendary Hollywood pilot Paul Mantz, (see the section at the end of this chapter) and flown by employees of his Paul Mantz Aerial Services for filming the flying sequences. The UC-78 "Bobcat", was painted with the Songbird name and the Flying Crown Ranch insignia.

The model used in the filming was built as the UC-78 and as the AT-17 "Bobcat" in the military configuration, as well as the T-50 in the civilian version.

At least two other T-50s are known to have been used for on-ground and in-the-cockpit scenes as well as a Beechcraft in one of the episodes. (Source: Proboards)

(Photo credit: Bill Larkins - Cessna T-50 NC67094, CC BY-SA 2.0, http s://commons.wikimedia.org/w/index.php?curid=29359024)

At the start of the war, Cessna obtained contracts to build the AT-17 Bobcat version of the aircraft for both Canada and the United States. According to Wikipedia, the AT-17, had a top speed of 195 mph, a cruise speed of 175 mph, and was used during World War II to fill the gap between single-engine trainers and twin-engine combat aircraft.

The T-50 was Cessna's first twin aircraft. The prototype was first flown in March of 1939, was approved for a Type Certificate in December of that year, and was adopted by the Army Air Force as an advanced multi-engine trainer in 1940, with the designation of AT-17.

In the military, the plane became known affectionately as the "Bamboo Bomber" due to its predominantly wooden airframe. For that reason it was also known as "Rhapsody in Glue". A version of the plane designated UC-78 was designed for cargo and transport.

The Royal Canadian Air Force ordered 1,190 planes from Cessna, and in the tradition of naming aircraft after birds, the plane was known in Canada as
the "Crane." The production run lasted until 1944 with a total of 5,402 produced. The last 368 aircraft, designated AT-17, were delivered to the U.S. Army Air Force.

The aircraft had a wingspan of 42 feet, was 33 feet long, and weighed just over 3500 pounds. The engine was listed as a Jacobs R-755. Cessna built the T-50 as civilian aircraft for the commercial transport market. It was constructed of wood and tubular steel and covered with fabric, thus the nickname "Bamboo Bomber".

According to ClassicWarbirds.net the T-50 was described as "a light-weight, low cost twin for personal use, where larger aircraft such as the Beech 18 would be too expensive. The T-50 and AT-17 are essentially the same airplane, configured for different purchasers.

Even before the end of the war, the USAAF and the RCAF began disposing of surplus T-50's, and FAA records show a total of 3,807 of various models were sold and converted to civil operation, all apparently registered in the U.S.

In some of the early Sky King show openings, even though they are in black and white, the color and trim of the plane with the familiar N67832 tail
number is different. There is a reason for that.

In the first production series, four different T-50 planes were painted with the N67832 tail number. Two were actually flown, one was used at the sound stage and the fourth was kept at Apple Valley Airport and used for taxiing, loading and unloading sequences.

There were at least four Bobcats used in the filming of the Sky King shows, all identified by the single name "Songbird".

One of the four, a UC-78B, one of the last batch ordered by the US-AAF, with the Cessna serial number 6117 and the YSAAF serial number 43-32179, was owned at one time by Paul Mantz Aerial Services and was provided for the show's filming, featured predominantly in the flying sequences of the first thirty-nine shows.

The history of that particular plane began in August of 1943 when it was delivered to the USAAF and spent most of its military career at Minter Army Airfield in Bakersfield, California. In 1946 it was sold as surplus by the War Assets Administration, then converted to a civilian configuration with a
factory modification kit, then registered as NC67832, which was changed to N67832 after June 14, 1948. Between 1946 and 1960 it had passed through no less than fifteen owners, including Mantz. Although the registration remains on file with the FAA, it has expired. The last owner is listed as Winifred Jo Ferro of Clinton, Missouri. The very first T-50, or pieces of it, are rumored to be somewhere in Missouri.

Between 1951 and 1956 (episodes 1 through 39), the first Songbird was a twin-engine Cessna T-50 Bobcat. The plane is white with the edges of the engines and the nose painted red.

The second Cessna Bobcat, bearing the number N68396 appears in episodes 5 (season 1), 24, 37 and 39 (season 2), shot between the end of 1955 and the first quarter of 1956. The Cessna UC-78B (s / n 43-32464), was registered N68311 after the war. This particular plane did not belong to Paul Mantz. Painted entirely in a dark color with a white stripe in the series, that plane was completely destroyed in 1965. In the credits of episodes 28 to 32 (season 2), released at the beginning of 1956, a different Cessna T-50 is viewed from the front, with a decoration very different from the usual "Songbird", with the edges of the engine hoods, the whole nose, and the windshields painted a very dark color.

More about Paul Mantz at the end of this chapter.

According to records I found, a T-50 plane with the N number NC4571N, later became N4571N, and joined the Sky King show in 1952. After the production of the first 19 episodes under Jack Chertok, the show was canceled. Then in 1956, Stuart and Darrell McGowan began production of a new series of shows for Nabisco. As part of the deal, the McGowans obtained stock footage of N67832 from the earlier episodes. However, Mantz was using that plane in the movie "the Steal Lady, so the McGowans found another plane, painted it a simpler version from the original, used different colors, and used it mostly for ground sequences and cockpit close,ups. That plane was serial number 3305, which had been delivered to the USAAF in December of 1942, at the Marfa Army Air Field in Texas, sold as surplus and registered as NC4571N. That plane also appears in the FAA registry under the ownership of Jon D. Larson, in Auburn, Washington. I tracked down Jon Larson in 2017 to confirm he owns that aircraft as well as another of the originals, N5378N, with serial number 4510. At this writing both registrations are still current. Larson also has an extensive collection of Sky King photos which he has displayed at Oshkosh events.

There are detectable differences between the planes used in the series. The original plane, N67832, that Paul Mantz owned, had Lycoming engines. By the time the McGowans obtained the rights to produce the show, Mantz was using that plane in the movie "the Steal Lady". The McGowans bought another surplus AT-17 and repainted it the same colors, but that second plane had Jacobson engines and no spinners on the propellers. That plane was serial number 3305.

In an interview, Ron Hagerthy, who played "Clipper" in the series, said a complete plane was used on the sound stage for entry and exit scenes. Its identification and history remain a mystery. Hagerthy also shared that a cabin/cockpit mock-up was used for close up photography. It may have been salvaged from scrap, because from what I have heard about the McGowans, they would not have gone to the expense of buying a whole plane only to tear it down for photo shoots. The budgets were tight.

(The Cessna UC-78 N67832, "Songbird" as it appeared in the television show)

This aircraft (s/n 6117 and s/n 43-32179, NC67832), was built in 1943, and was a former UC-78B sold by the War Assets Administration on November 18, 1946 to an individual from California. It had two other owners before being sold in August 1950, to Paul Mantz, who was technical adviser for the Sky King series in 1951 and 1952. It was flown during the filming by pilots employed by Paul Mantz Air Services, which was located at the Lockheed Air Terminal of Burbank, not at the Paul Mantz business. The plane was sold again in April 1954.

When Paul Mantz sold N67832, in April 1954, the plane changed owners three times in the same year, the last buyer keeping it until May 1956 when it sold for the small sum of $1,350 in Bakersfield, CA. It probably needed a lot of work after the shooting of season 2, with the replacement of the UC-78 by newer-model Cessna.

That first original plane passed through many hands in California, Colorado, and Missouri, where it was acquired in April 1960 by its more recent owner in Clinton, Missouri, where the plane appears to have been stored and disassembled.

There were several Cessna UC-78's with the "Songbird" markings. A white Bobcat reappears furtively in the episode of Season 3, "The haunted castle", which was first released on March 13, 1958.

According to Steve Brown, the landing gear in the T-50 had an electric motor and a bicycle chain running down to a gearbox. Sometimes that chain would stretch and it would go "bang-bang-bang" against the metal. At times, the gear would get winched, and it would blow the circuit breaker and you would have to hand-crank it from there. But one way or the other, the gear would still go into place.

Cessna 310B

The Cessna 310 is an American six-seat, low-wing, twin-engine monoplane that was produced by Cessna between 1954 and 1980. It was the first twin-engine aircraft that Cessna put into production after World War II. (Wikipedia)

Unit cost: $59,950 USD (1959)
Engine: Flat engine
Number built: 6,321
Produced: 1954–1980

First flight: January 3, 1953
Manufacturer: Cessna

Cessna produced a number of versions of the 310, from the 310-B to the 310-R which ended production in 1980.

A Wikipedia reference quoting an article "310 B Goes To Hollywood", includes a number of contradictions. The article places the Sky King Ranch as being located near Culver, California. In the show, the nearby town was Grover. It mentions the show aired locally on KAKE-TV Friday evenings at 6 pm and that the show was carried by 115 stations around the country. KAKE is the local station for Wichita, Kansas, where Cessna aircraft were built, which tells us where the article was written. The way it is written, the article could have been printed in a Cessna newsletter of the time, which would be the reason the original publication is so hard to find.

Also mentioned in the article is Jack Bledsoe, District Sales Manager for Cessna, Whitman Air Park and the Cessna dealership operated by Hank Coffin. Those mentions may also be clues to the source of the article.

Of course, much of the acting and close-ups took place on a sound stage with the use of mock-ups. The article describes a number of Songbird II stand-ins.

"Experimental people had a big part in the show" it said. "They cleaned up the old static test mock-up, dug up scrap antennas, doors, wheels, and an instrument panel - a list of things as long as your arm".

Assemblers on the 310 line back at Cessna reportedly did their part, supplying scrap cabin trim, a nose cap, glass, and other cabin fittings. Shipping crews boxed up the items, stenciled them for Hollywood, where filming personnel took over and reconstructed the 310 cabin for the show.

Just as there were several copies of the "General Lee" used in the Dukes of Hazard television show, Cessna provided three 310 aircraft for the production as well as stock footage of the aircraft in flight.

I've been informed that one of those original Sky King planes is now housed at the Smithsonian air museum and is periodically brought out for exhibit to the public. According to the company, Cessna filming used three Cessna 310 planes, one of which was used to film the aerial views.

The cockpit sequences were shot in a fuselage which was used for various tests at Cessna and then provided to the production site, where the cockpit was rebuilt in the studio. Trivia buffs with an eye for detail will notice the

V-shaped antenna (Com1, VOR and glide slope) sometimes appearing on the roof is different from the VHF antenna inclined towards the rear of the plane in flight.

N5348A was sold to the A-1 Iron & Metal Company of Alamada (CA) in October 1957, then to Huntair (October 1958), to California General Inc. (February 1959) and to the Cunningham Construction Company in 1962. That's where we lose track. According to some, the plane crashed sometime in 1957 shortly after the end of the shooting, but according to others, it was stolen in 1970 by drug traffickers. The plane was also said to have been destroyed on 8 August 1962 in Delano (CA), killing its owner B. Cunningham. The problem is that neither in 1957 nor in 1962 did the NTSB or FAA have any record of a Cessna 310 accident in California or elsewhere. The FAA canceled the plane's registration in 1970 when the owner did not respond to notifications from the FAA registration office in Oklahoma, and the N number was reassigned to a Cessna 320.

Steve Brown (Sky King Airport) told me the tail of that plane later turned up in Pennsylvania. The fate of the rest of the plane appears to be unknown.

Cessna 310B (N6635B)

Another Cessna 310B (s/n 35735) that appeared in the series, was built in 1958. Little is known about this plane, other than it was likely destroyed on landing on September 17, 1969, in Denton, Tx, after a trip from Ardmore, OK. According to some reports, it belonged to Viking Aero Service at the time. An accident matching the description appears in the NTSB reports. The N Number was later reassigned to a Beach aircraft.

Cessna 310D (N6817T)

A last Cessna 310 was used after the end of the shooting, to promote the series with a blue and light yellow decoration. It was used for events with Kirby Grant. It is a model 310-D, (s/n 3911, N6817T), built in 1960.

As it happens, that plane was once owned by Steven Brown whose flying school still operates from the Sky King Airport in Indiana. Steven Brown not only runs the airport and flying school but he sells airplanes. Some years back he sold several planes to a customer in Anchorage Alaska. He came back looking for more planes, but the only thing Brown had left was a model 310. Brown hired a pilot to deliver the plane to Alaska. The pilot liked it so much he never came back to Indiana.

After about six months the customer, Lee Bracher, called and told Brown, "Hey, I want to talk to you about this 310… it's got some history". Brown thought, "oh, boy, maybe it had been wrecked or something like that.…" Bracher went on, "I researched it and this is the same plane that they used" in the Sky King show". (Actually, it was never really used in a show, but it was used for those promotional appearances with Kirby Grant.)

Bracher later sold the plane. It remained for several years abandoned on the Nut Tree Airport in Vacaville, CA., until Paul Erikson, who was living in the area, bought it in 1981, restored it, and put it back to the original colors. Paul entered the plane at the annual Oshkosh event in Wisconsin and it won the Grand Champion.

I spoke with Paul Erickson by phone, and he shared that it took 10 years to finish the restoration. When he bought it, it was under the condition that the plane be restored and used. The only part that is not "original" is the interior. Paul couldn't deal with the 1957 Chevy look of gold trimmed leather so he opted for buckskin leather instead. The plane has about 800 hours on the meter. Like so many others, Paul traced his aviation inspiration to the Sky King program.

Steve Brown told me he went to see it in Oshkosh one year and claimed that Erikson wanted to sell it back to him. One Oshkosh visitor tried to tell Steve Brown that the plane on display is a "fake". Brown knew better, but he let it go. That plane is pictured in a photo was provided to me by David Vanderhoof, co-host of the UAV Digest and Airplane Geeks podcasts.

(Songbird III at Oshkosh. Photo courtesy of David Vanderhoof/Airpla-
neGeeks and

The UAV Digest Podcasts. Aircraft owned and restored and flown by Paul
Erickson)

Steven Brown described one promotional event where Cessna sent a plane, painted the familiar Flying Crown logo and "Songbird" name in washable paint. After the event, the decals were washed off and the plane returned to Cessna.

For budgetary reasons, the production used stock footage, sometimes mounted upside down with the numbers appearing with a mirror effect and not in the right place. The views behind the credits, and some repetitive passages (flights in the mountains, landings or takeoffs at the Flying Crown Ranch or in the countryside) were filmed with the first Cessna 310B (N5348A, "Songbird" written in light colors) and mixed with those of the N6635B ("Songbird" written in black). In the last episodes, the name "Songbird" appears written in two colors, gilded and black or even in black underlined white. In addition, the Songbird was mostly filmed from afar, which facilitated the substitution between the two. The last of the Songbirds used for the production was a 1960 Cessna 310D.

The Cessna UC-78 N68396 / 68311

Other Planes

Many episodes only show the Cessna UC-78 or the 310, but during the shooting many other planes were used. In episodes 33, 35, and 39 (season 2, March-April 1956), there is another Cessna, a model 170 (s/n 18188, NC2678V). Built in 1948, it was deleted from the registry in 2009. In "Dust of destruction" (episode 39), it is doubled by an Aeronca, (seen only in the front) in its role as an agricultural "crop duster".

The Cessna 170 N2678V

From the first episode, "Operation urgent" (April 1952), a number of planes and pilots were called into service. For example, a USAF officer piloted a North American NA-145 Navion, pictured below, (s / n NAV-4-22, N91132) with the American stars marking a military L-17. At last check this plane, one of the first produced in 1946, was still flying.

The North American Navion N91132

Another plane seen in the series was a Lockheed 12A Junior, belonging to Paul Mantz (N60775). Rumor has it that it was used to shoot a film about Amelia Earhart (who flew a Lockheed L.10 and not a L.12). Mantz had it re-registered in 1961, N16020, to tie it to Amelia. The plane was built in 1937 (s/n 1243, originally registered N18955) and was first delivered to Western Air Express in February 1938 before returning to Lockheed the following year. It was converted into a model 212, a militarized version, sold in Holland, with the installation of a machine gun turret, the location of which, concealed by a metal sheet, is perfectly visible on Fletcher Airline's plane. It then served as a training plane (s/n 212-13, NX18955). In June 1940 it was delivered to the RCAF (CF-BQX, then "7642"), Mantz bought it in 1946 (NC60775) and resold it in 1961. Its famous new registration number did not bring it luck because the plane was destroyed in a crash at Fort Irwin in the Tiefort Mountains on December 16th of the same year.

The Lockheed 12A N60775

The episode "Sky Robbers" (December 28, 1958), was shot partly on the Whiteman airport, south of San Fernando. In that episode, Penny participates in an air race with a dark (unidentifiable) Culver Dart G that appeared in "The Round of the Dawn" (1957). Extracts from that film were used to show the racers turning around the towers.

Gloria Winters as "Penny" in front of her Culver Dart

In another episode, we also see a Beech D18S (s/n A-136, N44647) that belonged to United Distilleries between 1949 and 1960, before being acquired by Florida Airmotive. This plane was transformed with a tricycle train in 1963 (N187R). Since 2000 it has been based in Hawaii. In the background in the episode, there are several other aircraft including two Douglas DC-3s, one Aeronca, and one Bellanca 14-12 (s/n 1034, N25312) still flying in California at last check.

The Beech D18S N44647

The episode "Double Trouble" the Cougar (December 29, 1957) the reservist Sky King pilots a Grumman F9F-6. Its tail number "7L" (in 1957) is a plane from the Naval Air Reserve Training Unit of the Naval Base Los Alamitos, CA., where the scene was filmed. The plane is also marked "US Navy Los Alamitos", on the back. Before the Songbird lands, we are even shown an aerial view of the base with its two parallel landing strips, 22/4 and not "27/9", as announced by the tower. Sky's look-alike parks the Songbird just in front of the control tower. In the background, are a Consolidated PB4Y-2 Privateer, a Douglas Skyraider, and several Lockheed P2V-7 Neptunes. The Cougar was armed with four 20 mm guns, with which Sky "shoots" the Songbird, which would have had the immediate effect of totally blowing it up, but in the scene, the 20 mm shells turn into "peaceful" 7.7 mm balls that make only a few holes in the fuselage of the Cessna.

Grumman F9F-6 Cougar (BuNo 128158)

In the episode "Terror cruise" (11/01/1959), Sky King lands the Song-bird on an aircraft carrier. The scene was reconstructed by editing and mixing several excerpts from US Navy footage. Sky King contacts the USS "Good Man Richard" (CVA-31), to make his approach to the USS "Boxer" (the code CV-21 is seen upside down on deck). Sky then finds himself behind the USS "Kersage" (CV-33), where the security barrier is deployed. On the bridge of the "Good Man Richard", there's a McDonnell F2H-3 Banshee, "408" (BuN.126484) of the VF-213.

In "Bounty hunters" (01/01/1959), traffickers use an Aeronca L-16A (s/n 7EC503, N7454B). Built in 1956, that plane was removed from the FAA registers in 1977. It also appears in one of the last episodes, "A Mickey for Sky" (01/22/1959).

The Aeronca L-16A N7454B

In "Money has wings" (01/01/1959) as the "Songbird" lands at night with the Beech 18 "N44647" from "Sky robbers", with the engine oddly starting with the sound of the Lycoming R-680-9. At the small airport (Apple Valley airport?), there are several planes in the background: a Beech 18, two Douglas DC-3 / C-47s, including the C-47B Wien Alaska Airlines (s/n 25768, s / n 43-48507, N91014), Douglas B-18 Bolo civil, Beech 35 Bonanza, Cessna 172 (N4170F), two North American TB-25 civilian North American Navions, a rare Longren Centaur (a civil conversion of the Convair L-12, seen close to the Wellman office), as well as amphibians: a Republic Seabee, a Grumman G-44 Widgeon, a Consolidated Catalina PBY-5.

The Douglas C-47 N91014 from WIEN. In the background on the right, a PBY-5.

In "The crystal trap", there is a Cessna T-50 bearing the false registration number "N68396". When Sky King takes it down with a rifle, it first turns into a biplane, Stearman or Travel Air, and when it crashes, it becomes the Travel Air 10-D (s/n 10-2008, NC414N).

In "A Mickey for Sky", the young Mickey arrives on a United Airlines DC-4.

Beech 35 Bonanza - N3306V - Sequence mounted in reverse: the door is actually on the right

In "Designing woman" (June 14, 1952), a Beech 35 Bonanza (s/n D765, N3306V), piloted by Clipper, bears the logo of the Flying Crown Ranch. This particular aircraft, built in 1947, was still flying in Texas several decades later. A farmer pilots another Beech A35 Bonanza (s/n D1616, N595B) in episode 29, "Rustlers on wheels" (5/03/1956). In "Uninvited death" (December 6, 1956), the same plane is seen stationed next to a small monoplane Ercoup 415-C. That Bonanza was destroyed January 20,1993, in Tulare, in a fatal accident while it belonged to a rental company.

The Bell 47 as it appeared in "Giant Eagle"

A few helicopters appeared in the TV series, but were filmed on the ground. A Bell 47, one of the very first models of the series with wheels, makes an appearance in "Giant Eagle" (October 18, 1952). In "Mystery horse" (December 29,1957), when a forest fire threatens a misled thoroughbred, another Bell 47 is seen in the background.[1]

WACO

According to a comment attributed to Gloria Winters, Kirby Grant started his flying career in a 1929 WACO tail-wheel biplane. While the WACO aircraft was not involved in the television show, it may have played a part in Kirby Grant's attraction to aviation.

So for that reason, we'll briefly mention that historic aircraft. It's also an aircraft with an interesting history.

Although the company had several names throughout its history, beginning with the Weaver Aircraft Company, the name most associated with the plane is WACO. The name could come from the initials of the Weaver

---

1. (Source for much of the above, translated from aeromovies.fr)

Aircraft Company... or not, depending on which account you read. Some sources say that the name comes from a field near Troy, Ohio, which is where the company moved from its beginnings in Lorain and Medina, Ohio when Mr. Weaver left the company.

The "WA" in WACO rhymes with "Water", and so WACO is pronounced "WAH-COH". The WACO, was named for the manufacturer, Weaver Aircraft Company, and not for the town in Texas.

(Photo: WACO aircraft)

There were several different WACO models built by Weaver Aircraft Company in Ohio, from the early open cockpit to a 3-seat, closed cabin model and it eventually morphed into a mono-wing glider. Some models of the WACO were designed and never built, some, only a handful were made. For many of the WACO models, only 3 or 4 ever flew.

There were models used for mail and military use. The early models featured a tubular metal fuselage but wings made of wood and covered with cotton fabric.

The most prolific was the WACO Model 9, with 270 built, including the Miss Pittsburgh, which was discovered and restored by OX 5 Aviation

Pioneers, and is now displayed at the Pittsburgh International Airport, Landside Terminal.

The WACO 9 featured a stall speed of just 32 miles per hour, due to the large wing surface of the double-wing, bi-plane design, but could still reach an altitude of 5,000 feet, cruise at 72 mph with a maximum speed of 100 mph with its OX5 engine. It was even equipped for EDO floats. Some surviving WACO aircraft can also be seen at air shows around the world.

(Photo Source: Wikipedia)

The WACO lives on in the R/C (radio control) world, with the Horizon Hobby E-flite UMX Waco BL BNF that you can see at many AMA model aircraft club fields, powered by an electric motor. (Photo Source: Horizon Hobby)

Paul Mantz

Paul Mantz, whose company provided the plane and pilot for the first series of the Sky King show, was an American aviator who became the most renowned "stunt flier" in movies of the mid-twentieth century.

Mantz was quoted as saying "I'm not a stunt pilot, I'm a precision pilot".

The son of a school principal, Mantz grew up in Redwood City, California and developed a fascination with flying as a boy. He joined the Air Corps as a cadet and was a brilliant student pilot, but he was discharged after buzzing a train full of high-level officers. After a brief period of commercial flying, Mantz took up the more lucrative career of stunt flying for the film industry. He quickly proved himself willing and capable of tackling stunts considered by other pilots to be too dangerous. He formed United Air Services, Ltd., providing planes and pilots for aerial stunts and photography for all the studios.

During the Second World War, Mantz served as commanding officer of the Army Air Corps' First Motion Picture Unit, delivering hundreds of training films and documentaries on the air war. He developed a number of camera and aeronautical innovations to improve aerial photography, and continued as a stunt flyer, a director of aerial photography, and a supplier of aircraft and pilots for the movies for two decades after the war.

Mantz also formed a flying school and racing partnership with Amelia Earhart and was technical adviser on her ill-fated round-the-world flight, but was dismissed before her second, fatal attempt. Earhart was named co-respondent in Mantz's 1936 divorce.

Mantz shot the aerial footage for *This Is Cinerama* (1952) and other early Cinerama travelogues.

Mantz won the Bendix Trophy airplane races three years running, 1946-1948.

In 1946, Mantz purchased 475 surplus bombers and fighters for $55,000, anticipating a postwar boom in war movies. He converted one of these, a B-25 bomber he christened "The Smasher", into a state-of-the-art flying camera platform that he would use for the next 20 years.

Mantz was the first pilot to perform the stunt of flying an airplane through an open hangar, in *Air Mail* (1932).

To get the attention of producers who would not hire him, he performed an "outside loop" - a loop where the plane is upside-down at the bottom of the circle - in July, 1930, using a plane he specially modified for the stunt.

According to Bob Fish of the Associated Airtanker Pilots, Danville California, Mantz installed a rubber bladder in the bomb bay of his WWII TBM Avenger and filled it with water, thus becoming the first to demonstrate the incredible value of aerial technology in wildfire suppression.

In the movie *12 O'clock High* in 1949, Mantz was paid $4,500. (Source: IMDB.com)

In 1965, he came out of retirement to fly a plane for *The Flight of the Phoenix* (1965) and was killed in a crash. Pallbearers at his funeral included his friend ,James Stewart; General James Doolittle; director, John Ford; and test pilot, Chuck Yeager.

The Later Years

K irby Grant was bit of a circus star. When Kirby was not shooting his television show, he was a special guest star on many different circuses. He traveled with the Carson and Barnes Circus from 1965 to 1967.

Sky King in Person! Poster for Carson and Barnes Circus (circa '60s).
"Sky King" in a personal appearance poster for the Carson and Barnes Circus in the 1960s

A quote from that time: "We did numerous shows with him throughout the years. I can tell you this, he loved every moment of being around circus performers and even got into some of the acts.......If you let him. Kirby Grant was a fine man." [1]

The Sky King shows continued to play in reruns from 1959 to 1966, but Grant and the other actors received no residuals. So Kirby had to do other things. He and Gloria Winters were in demand for personal appearances at fairs and aviation events.

Kirby Grant is listed as the recording artist on two Wizard Records singles, #245-A "Loving Time" and 245-B "Letter from Tina" circa 1970. You might find a copy on eBay.[2]

The photo below was captioned: "Actor Kirby Grant, CBS TV's 'Sky King' star, poses with Nashville-based songstress Donna Darlene at downtown First American Bank building, May 1, 1967. Grant was in town to make some country music records with Wizard Records. Darlene would join him in a duet on one of the records."

(Photo rights purchased from Tennesseean newspaper)

Kirby Grant went to work for a Mr. Adams in December of 1969. Adams was president of Lifetime Security Life Insurance in Denton, Texas. He said he hired Kirby because Kirby was "down on his luck," living in a trailer park with Carolyn and Kip. He thought Kirby would be a great asset. He described Kirby as a "very good man" with "a lot of integrity" who "really pulled us up" ("us" referring to the company). Kirby went to Florida to improve the company's situation there on behalf of that company. According to my sources, Adams later got into trouble with a real estate deal in Arkansas. Kirby was not involved in that situation in any way, but he was once again out of work.

1. (Source: www.thecircusblog.com/?p=27167)

2. (Source: alchetron.com/Kirby-Grant-1367611-W)

As Carolyn related in her tapes, the couple lived in 19 places in California. In 1971, long after the end of the Sky King series, Kirby, Carolyn, and son Kip moved to Florida. Kendra seems to have inherited her talent for music from her father. She stayed behind in California, but before they left, her parents bought her a baby grand piano. Every Christmas, Kendra sent music tapes to the family. Daughter Kristen lived in Texas for a time and later moved to Florida.

In California, everything has Spanish names. As Kirby and Carolyn looked at the map of Central Florida, they saw the town of Oviedo. They looked it up and found that Oviedo, Florida has a "sister city" in Spain. When they got to Oviedo, the mayor, who also happened to be the local barber, introduced himself to Kirby and said "Welcome to Oviedo!" He pronounced it "Oh-VEE-duh", as the locals do. Kirby, was clearly disappointed. He said, "I thought it was "Oh-vee-AY-doh." The city's name comes from capital city of the Principality of Asturias in northern Spain.

That wasn't the last time Kirby was to be disappointed by the local pronunciations. Kirby and Carolyn were invited to nearby Monte Verde to judge a beauty and talent contest. The dean of the school welcomed them with "Welcome to" Mont-VERD". The locals shorten the original Portuguese name from four syllables down to just two.

Kirby was a popular guest speaker with civic and business groups around the Central Florida area. As Kirby gave various talks he would recall his pronunciations of Oviedo, Monte Verde and Kissimmee. During a talk to a local group in Sanford, he remarked "I guess there's not much they can do with a town with the name 'Sanford' ." Not so. I lived in Sanford for a time and I found many locals who could turn the name into three-syllables: "SAY-ann-ferd".

When the family moved to Winter Springs, they attended the Episcopal Church in Longwood, Florida. Kirby was active there as well, singing in the choir. But as time went on, as Carolyn told it, he and the choir director didn't get along. Kirby would bring his choir robe home and hang it up. He would later reconsider and try again, tangle with the director once again and the robe would go back in the closet.

It was that same church that would later hold the memorial services after Kirby's death.

I had worked as a film editor for various television stations. It was during those later years of syndication in the 1970's. I was hired by the late Bob

Yde and TVSCO to clean and process the 16 mm black and white Sky King television films for distribution (syndication). The customers were television and Cable companies. I was also working for a local radio station at the time and I met Kirby when I did an interview with him for the station.

The Great American Air Show

Bob Yde was aware that Kirby was "down on his luck", even trying to sell some of his Sky King memorabilia. Bob had the idea of featuring Kirby as the main attraction for air shows staged around the country. Kirby was to be a key attraction, acting as the announcer for the various events.

In my view, Bob Yde was the ultimate producer, and came up with the idea for the "Great American Air Show". There have been many air shows with that title, but this was different. Bob went to a number of evets to see how it was done, and then he reinvented the airshow. It wasn't just any air show, this one was choreographed, from the minute people came through the fence. It was more than just an air show, where the pilots flew by once in a while. There is a video of one of the events presented in Africa that can be found on YouTube.

Bob Yde got in touch with John Schoop, who owned the Dukes of Dixieland, in New Orleans. John supplied a lot of the music and his musicians actually recorded music just for the airshow. Bob was the voice of Air Show Control and Kirby Grant was the announcer, with more voices coming from the pilots in the cockpit. The pilots would call out their maneuvers, which was new for the time, and the music added to the package. Bob even went on the Larry King show in Miami to promote the first event in Fort Lauderdale. The Great American Airshow was created strictly as a vehicle for Kirby Grant. (Source, my interview with Cassie Yde).

Bob hired me to work in the sound truck for one of the airshows. Bob Yde also hired Walt Pierce as one of the pilots to participate in the airshows.

Kirby Grant, Sandy and Walt Pierce

The air shows began rehearsing in October of 1975. They went "on the road" in Fort Lauderdale in January, then on to Fort Worth and California, to Nevada and back to Las Cruces, then to Dallas and a show at Sarasota, Florida around Easter. (Source: My interviews with Walt Pierce)

Wing walking was still a "thing" with stunt pilots even into the 1960s. Walt and his then-wife Sandy bought a Stearman in 1968, but by then, as Walt says, "they were all gone but Richard Lybarger"... who was soon killed in a freak accident at his own airport in Iowa. That left his wing walker without a wing to walk on. So, Walt worked with Richard's "girl", Patti Deck in Chicago in 1971. At the later Florida shows, Walt convinced Sandy to be the wing walker on their Stearman. Walt retired to Sebring, Florida, and told me he goes to the annual Sun N Fun event in Lakeland just to show he's still around. Walt Pierce had so many stories to tell.

Walt told me the WACO was used as the primary trainer for "barnstormers", but it was not an easy plane to learn to fly. Walter flies a Stearman, but he is very familiar with the WACO of that day.

As Walt described it,

(Photo: Walt Pierce and his Stearman at Avon Park Airport, 2017 - Photo by Tim Trott)

"My goodness, people learned to fly in this thing? I don't see how people went from hardly knowing how to drive a car, crawl in this thing and go flying. It was very forgiving because it was slow. It was light and slow, but you had to pay attention to which way the wind was blowing. You had to compensate for the crosswind. You had to have it all figured out what you were going to do before you got there. The saving grace of a plane like the WACO 9 was [that] it had tail skids. If you put the main wheels down and just pull the stick all the way back... they were tail-heavy airplanes... Once you had the main wheels down and were bouncing along over gopher holes, if you forced the tail skid into the turf, you pretty much had control. When they started to pave runways the skid was replaced by a tail wheel. Otherwise, you would spend all your time replacing the skid plate. The landing strips went from grass pasture to more stable surfacing with a foundation of limestone. But it didn't help you slow down like it would with grass."

"They were unstable and they didn't have a lot of power, and you really had to move all the controls [in] the right direction or it would look like somebody trying to fly a comedy act or something".

The first time Walt met Kirby Grant was in 1973 at the Sanford Airport near Orlando. Walt could not believe he was actually talking to "Sky King" and would be working with him. Especially out west in places like El Paso. Sometimes 10 to 20 people would circle around Kirby by the picket fence, not believing they were talking to the "real" Sky King.

Walt Pierce said that when he and Kirby would talk flying, Kirby avoided anything technical. Kirby would switch the conversation to what they were doing at the time. He skirted around anything about himself and his flying.

Walter Pierce tells about the time one of the air shows featured the Navy Blue Angels. Some of those pilots went out of their way to come over to say how impressionable it was to have seen Sky King on television. Kirby was affected by that reaction, pushed his hat back and told them "I had no idea I had that much impact. Thank you for sharing that with me". Kirby Grant was always overwhelmed by the enthusiasm toward him and the impact he had made on so many people and flying.

Walt Pierce counts himself as one of those kids who watched the Sky King show on television and became interested in flying. The month before he turned 16, in December of 1955, Walt took his first flying lesson and earned his license in January of 1958. He associated with pilots of the 1920's and 1930's and got into aerobatic flying, with his Stearman biplane.

Later on, Bob Yde also wanted to build a nightclub singing act around Kirby's musical talents. A band was formed in the Mt. Dora area, and they put together a collection of songs, but it didn't work out. I was told the problem was that while Kirby's singing voice was still in good form, he had difficulty memorizing the lyrics.

Sky King Youth Ranch

Some reports (People magazine) stated that the Sky King Youth Ranches of America in Seminole County was "founded by" Kirby and Carolyn Grant". A copy of Kirby Grant's hand-typed resume lists "Founder of Sky King Youth Ranch". However, according to Kip Grant, that's not what really happened. Public records show that in July of 1969, two years before Kirby Grant moved to Florida, a group formed the non-profit Seminole All Youth Shelter, Inc.. The purpose was to provide homes and guidance for troubled teens. The original group encountered various difficulties. They decided it might help if they could convince Kirby Grant to lend his name to the project. In May of 1975, the ranch became Sky King Youth Ranches of America. The Florida non-profit corporation, listing Kirby's home address as the "principal address". The ranch was located on 15 acres near Chuluota, Florida. The corporation consisted of Kirby, his wife, Carolyn, and three other members. However, there were continued financial issues and disputes among board members. Some of those issues may have had something to do with Kirby's problems with "details" like keeping receipts and filing forms.

There was a Sanford Evening Herald newspaper article titled "Sky King Shakeup". It said that Kirby Grant said fellow board members did not agree with his policies. It quoted Kirby as saying "I founded the organization and I plan to keep it up". There were questions about state licensing and placement of foster children. There was also a matter of the total number of children under the organization's care. At various times, at various locations, the organization was responsible for between 16 and 45 boys and girls.

Kirby's heart was in the right place but it didn't work out. The State of Florida forced the project to be "involuntarily dissolved" in December of 1982. The project was briefly revived in 1984 as Seminole Youth Ranch, Inc., but was voluntarily dissolved again in 2013. (Sources include Sunbi z.com)

By all accounts, Kirby Grant's interest in the youth ranch was not financial. That was the same as his participation in fundraising activities for the American Heart Association. At a time when Jerry Lewis was splitting the funds raised in the annual telethons, Kirby took no compensation and often paid his own expenses

Kirby's interest in supporting American Heart Association events had one personal aspect. A severe heart attack in 1978 led to three bypass operations. They replaced the aortic valve. He had a choice of having a pig valve or a metal valve. He chose the porcine valve. As Carolyn described "At 70 years old, he came through with flying colors". There had been troubles in the marriage in the past but Carolyn said in the years after the surgery they had become closer than ever.

I visited Kirby at his home in Winter Springs just after that operation. It was then that Kirby told me about the book he intended to write, to be titled, "Out of the Blue". Those were the words the announcer would proclaim at the opening of the old television show.

Just six weeks after the surgery Kirby had promised a personal appearance for the board of the Orange County Sportsman's Association. He was determined to keep his promise. He had lost some weight and was a little weak, and he had to sit down.

But... they had a "hog-calling" contest... and Carolyn knew what Kirby was going to do. "Kirby, you're not going to do that!" But he was, and he did, and he took a turn at the microphone.

After an extended recovery, Kirby took a job as a goodwill ambassador for Florida Festival at Sea World in Orlando in 1979. He held that position until 1985, before taking on a similar job at Cypress Gardens. At both jobs, co-workers remembered that many times people would say to Kirby "I'm a pilot because of you".

Photo credit: Florida Festival, Orlando, Florida

In November 1981, Bob Rolli hosted a "singing and dancing" party at the Private I Restaurant and club in honor of Kirby's 70th birthday. They played one of the old TV shows at the party and Kirby sang a couple of old songs. By all accounts, Kirby was looking "trim and young". That was just three years before his untimely death.

Kirby had met with astronauts several days prior to the last successful Challenger launch. They had a reception at a hotel where Kirby met with some of the astronauts. The next morning he was to have breakfast with some of the astronauts, but he had a meeting at Sea World, so he had to come back home.

The Orlando Sentinel newspaper reported that Kirby had been invited "by a friend" to the VIP stands to view what was to be the last successful launch of the space shuttle Challenger. The source of that comment was Arnold Richmond, chief of visitor services at Kennedy Space Center.

I'm told that five of the seven astronauts on that last successful Challenger mission said they were inspired by the "Sky King" TV show. Carolyn Grant said that Kirby was "elated" before leaving for the launch the next morning.

(STS-61-A Crew, compliments of NASA)

At 8 am on October 30th, 1985, while driving to the shuttle launch, Kirby, then 73, was attempting to pass another vehicle on State Road 50. Four miles west of Titusville, a car he was passing pulled into his path. Kirby reportedly swerved to avoid a collision, then swerved back across the road and ran into a ditch. On impact, Kirby was thrown through the passenger window and clear of the car, into about three feet of water. A newspaper account said Roy Walters of Orlando stopped to help and pulled Kirby out of the water. According to Kirby's son Kip, his father was briefly revived at Jess Parrish Memorial Hospital in Titusville. Less than an hour later, however, he was pronounced dead. The initial cause of death was listed as drowning, but his heart condition could have been a factor.

The driver of the other car did not stop and from what I can find has never been identified or found. Back then, Highway 50 between Orlando and Titusville was a two-lane roadway. There was a newspaper report of a suit filed in Brevard County Circuit Court. That suit contended the state highway department had failed to build a guard rail along that section of road, even though its own guidelines required one. (Sources include The Orlando Sentinel, October 31, 1985)

By strange coincidence, the name of the Florida Highway Patrol officer who investigated the accident Mike Kirby.

About 10 am that morning, two highway patrolmen and a neighbor came to the house in Winter Springs to tell Carolyn and the family about the accident. The next day Carolyn Grant received this telegram (actually a government TWX) from Ronald Reagan:

```
10-31-85-TWX-GOVT          WHITE HOUSE, D.C.

OCT 31

MRS. CAROLINE GRANT        60-38 SHI-O-AH BOULEVARD       WINTER SPRINGS, FL  32708


NANCY AND I ARE VERY SADDENED BY KIRBY'S DEATH.  WE KNOW THAT HIS LOSS IS A

PAINFUL BURDEN FOR YOU BUT WE HOPE THAT YOU ARE CONSOLED BY KNOWING THAT HIS

MULTITUDE OF FANS WILL REMEMBER HIM WITH GREAT AFFECTION.  KIRBY WAS AN

INSPIRATION TO AMERICAN YOUTH AND YOU CAN TAKE GREAT PRIDE IN HIS ACCOMPLISHMENT

WE WILL KEEP YOU IN OUR PRAYERS AND WE SEND OUR CONDOLENCES.


                   RONALD REAGAN
```

(Source: Tim Trott, from materials provided by Carolyn Grant for this project)

At his passing, Kirby Grant Hoon, Jr., left behind his wife, three children and five grandchildren. A tombstone marks his burial site at Missoula Cemetery, Missoula County, Montana. Kirby Grant's father, Kirby Grant Hoon, Sr., who had passed away just a few years earlier in 1981, is buried in the same cemetery. Missoula City Cemetery, established in 1884, is one of the oldest operating cemeteries. The city of Missoula purchased the cemetery in 1901.

Carolyn Grant said that she took solace in the fact that Kirby "did die with his boots on". That's what she related to her friend and Terra Haute real estate agent Zoe Parks.

The memorial service for Kirby was held November 3rd at Christ Episcopal Church in Longwood. The church, north of Orlando, is the same church where Kirby had those "differences" with the choir director. It was a simple service, held outside, with a picture of Kirby provided by Sea World. Kip Grant remembers there was a large crowd in attendance. The crowd was such that it was necessary to ask local police to help with traffic control.

Someone flew a Cessna 310 over the church where the funeral service was being held. I have not been able to determine the identity of the pilot who honored Kirby Grant with that flight. A flight instructor at Sanford Airport at the time, Wayne Ceynowa, suggested some possibilities. I have not been able to learn the name of that pilot.

Sea World had wanted to have the Navy do a fly-by but decided against it. Cypress Gardens and Sea World flew their flags at half-mast in honor of Kirby's passing. Deaths that same year included Rock Hudson, Orson Wells, Yul Brynner, Phil Silvers, band leaders Nelson Riddle and Kay Kyser. Also Jaguar car company founder Sir William Lyons, Hostess Twinkie inventor James A. Dewar and Tex Williams. Hectar Boirdi, the founder of Boy-Ar-Dee Foods died that year along with Henry Cabot Lodge, Sam Ervin of Watergate Hearing fame and Margaret Hamilton, who played the Wicked Witch of the West opposite Judy Garland in the Wizard of Oz. That was also the year Karen Ann Quinlan died after 10 years in a coma. Charles Richter of the Richter Scale and E.B. White of Charlotte's Web also passed away that year.

Myths and factual errors seemed to follow Kirby Grant. One internet report listed the highway as the 528 Bee Line. A Terra Haute newspaper ad by a local bank claimed that Kirby had died in a small plane crash and listed the wrong year. That was also incorrect.

The newspaper clipping you see here was sent to me by Carolyn Grant. The clipping contains a number of factual errors. Note the last paragraph. Surely you would think there were enough people in Terra Haute who knew the facts. But as we quickly learned in researching for this book, you really can't believe everything you read about Sky King.

KIRBY ''SKY KING'' GRANT

Terre Haute National Bank tribute advertisement with incorrect information

Carolyn Grant passed away in her sleep a few years later in 1989. She was visiting the Louisiana home of Larry Tate, a family friend.

One thing that became very clear as I worked on this project. When Kirby Grant stepped out of the role of Sky King, he wore the white hat for the rest of his life. Whether the iconic hat was on his head or not. Kip Grant told me that his father made it a point to never smoke a cigarette around the "fans". That began well before the health concerns about smoking. Kirby always tried to maintain that "good-guy" white hat image, and there are many examples.

Steve Brown now operates his father's Brown Flying School at the Sky King Airport in Indiana. When I visited him, he described Kirby by saying "You'd never meet a finer guy. He came here and dedicated the airport. It was in August and it was hot. I remember that, and he was standing in the office, we didn't have air conditioning, and there was just a line of people, just one after another, going through there, getting autographs, and him standing there signing them. Sweat running off of him. Later my dad said, Kirby, I need to pay you. Kirby said, no sir, you're not about to." More about the Sky King Airport in the next chapter.

That's pretty much the way Kirby was described by those who knew him.

Kirby Grant grew up in Montana. A PBS production Back Roads of Montana produced a tribute to Kirby Grant. If you find it on YouTube, the Sky King segment is 7:55 into program number 23.   [3]

Backroads of Montana - University of Montana (umt.edu)

Kirby Grant remained amazed at the fans who were inspired by his Sky King television character. They told him so at air shows, at his job at Florida Festival or Sea World, at the many public appearances and speaking events, to his meeting with the Challenger astronauts. However quaint it may seem now, the writing and acting on the show were probably consistent with the times. But something else was also consistent: the good guys, in the white hats, always won the day. It really was, after all, a kid's show, and a lot of kinds took inspiration from Sky King.   From the movies to the television series and beyond, Kirby Grant never really took off that white hat. That's just who he was, and that says it all.

Image Source: Wikipedia commons

The Flying Cowboy

Here are some examples of the Sky King folklore:

"In real life, Kirby Grant, the actor who played Sky King, was a real pilot and rancher, and until he died in 1985, his ranch was in Valley Center."

'Sky King' star landed in Valley Center" The Way We Were -By Vincent Nicholas Rossi - June 11, 2006

"Just south of the intersection of Lake Wohlford Road and Valley Center Road is the remnant of an airstrip. According to Bob Lerner of the Valley Center History Museum, this was Grant's private strip. Grant's home was at the end of the airstrip, fronting on Valley Center Road."

Kirby Grant did not own a "private airstrip." He did not own the house at the end of the airstrip fronting Valley Center Road. [1]

One website says the Sky King TV program ran on Saturday mornings. In fact, it was on Saturday mornings only *after* moving to CBS.

There was a story going around that Kirby Grant had claimed to own a T-50. The details included Jacobs engines, Hamilton Standard props, and no spinners. The report said that Kirby had sold the plane after discovering it suffered from spar rot, a common issue with that model. It's not known when that would have been. We don't know who made up that story or why. Wear and tear on the spar of the T-50 was among the reasons the McGowans were looking for a replacement. But Kirby certainly could not afford to keep an airplane in his retirement years, and had no use for one.

Sky King Airport

Herman Brown met Kirby Grant in 1959 through a mutual friend. Herman Brown owned Brown Flying School near where Carolyn Gillis grew up in Terra Haute. Brown built a new private airport in what had once been a soybean field, five miles north of Terre Haute. During a visit, he told Kirby about the new airport, and Kirby suggested that it be named Sky King Airport. Brown liked the idea, so Kirby made a few contacts, and Nabisco granted permission to use the name Sky King Airport. He may have only had to pass it by Nabisco because one source indicated that Nabisco sold or gave Kirby the rights to "Sky King" in 1959.

Herman Brown flew Kirby Grant in the Songbird III to the new Sky King Airport from Hulman Airport for the airport dedication in August of 1962, . As Carolyn described it, there were "thousands of people" there. The Brown Flight School is still in business, training pilots after more than 50 years. FAA charts officially show the designation 3I3 for Sky King Airport. The plane that Cessna flew from the factory to the airport for the grand opening was N2922R. The Browns had ended up with that same

---

1. (Source: http://legacy.sandiegouniontribune.com/uniontrib/2006 0611/news_m1m11history.html)

airplane and one just like it. When they brought 22R, it was a kind of a Burgundy color, and the one they bought later (23R) was blue and gray.

(Photo of Kirby Grant and Herman Brown, courtesy of Steven and Amy Brown. The building behind is the office of Sky King Airport)

I interviewed Steven and Amy Brown in 2017.

Steven Brown: "We had the dedication at our airport first. And Kirby had been talking to them (Cessna), and Cessna brought a brand new 310 from Wichita, with two pilots, a sales representative, and somebody else, to Terra Haute, to our airport; we went to Hulman first. My dad had a guy put Songbird on the nose and the flying crown logo on the side of the airplane. And then Kirby was in the airplane, and they flew it into our (Sky King) airport. (it was the Cessna people, Herman Brown, and Kirby in the plane). It was parked out in front, and we had probably … they had an estimate of three thousand people that came here that day. They had a guy taking a lot of pictures; they had a dedication, had a Congressman there."

(Photo of Kirby Grant at the grand opening of Sky King Airport, courtesy of Steve and Amy Brown)

"I got to know Kirby, he was back here at Terra Haute a lot.... I think it was in 1985, my dad had taken a guy, from the television station, a news announcer, and taught him to fly, free, and they televised the whole thing, from start to finish. They did it in a 172, and they often had a cameraman in the back. I remember when, they did the stalls, the cameraman didn't want to go through that, so I went out and flew the cameraman in another airplane, right next to them while they were going up doing stalls, and he took pictures of that. The day the guy soloed, Kirby was here in town, and he came out, I got a video of it, they shot a picture of the guy taxiing up in the airplane, and Kirby going out there and congratulating

him on his first solo, and Kirby (autographed) his log book."
(Photos courtesy of Amy Brown, Brown Flying School)

When the local TV station wanted some promotional shots, Steve would put Kirby in the left seat of Steve's Cessna 310. The left seat is the pilot's set, just as it was in the TV show. When they made a low pass for the camera, Steve bent down so the camera couldn't see him in the right seat. After landing, Steve would get out before the photo crew reached the plane.

When Steve Brown described Kirby Grant, he said, "you'd never meet a finer guy. He came here and dedicated the airport. It was August, and it was hot... (Kirby) was standing in the office, we didn't have air conditioning, and there was a line of people, one after another, going through there, getting autographs, and him standing there signing them. Sweat was running off him." Later, Steven's dad told Kirby, "I need to pay you," and Kirby said, "No, sir, you're not about to."

Flying in the Brown family is not limited to Steven and his dad. Everybody but Steven's sister learned to fly, and she could even navigate pretty well. His dad and mother flew, his dad's first wife flew, and Steven's sister's two children learned to fly. Steven never had a job that didn't involve flying; he learned from his dad and soloed when he was only 12 years old. He only quit flying jets when he reached age 64.

The airport suffered a tornado in 2011, which destroyed the original office building, hangar, and Brown's home on the side of the airport. Herman Brown passed away in 2011 at 91. An online reference claims that Herman Brown owned Weaver Aircraft at one time. Steven Brown assures us that was never the case. But they did own a WACO aircraft at one time, they have a friend who restores WACO aircraft in nearby Greenwood, and they are a part of the WACO Aircraft club. I found them at the WACO table in the Vintage Aircraft hanger at the Oshkosh Airshow one year.

The Great Idea That Never Was

"These sales guys from Cessna, they saw that, and we didn't have any air show, that was all it was, and they said "that guy and that airplane, drew all that many people from that town, that day, out there to that airport, so that's when they invited my dad out to Cessna. What they were planning on doing ... it was almost a done deal.. They were going to give Kirby a new airplane, with Songbird III on a 310. They were going to go around and set up with the dealers, distributors, and stuff, around the country, and they would do the promotional thing prior to that, and then he would fly in, and they figured that would be a hell of a draw." (Steven Brown)

As the story goes, Kirby Grant went to the Cessna factory in Wichita, Kansas. They took a bunch of pictures of Kirby going through the factory as if he was picking out the parts of the airplane. It was a great promotional concept. The guys, likely sales staff, at the factory put the whole thing together. Kirby was going to actually go to work for Cessna. But Cessna had an advertising company, Gardener Advertising. Their home base in St. Louis. The ad agency was under contract with Cessna. Since they didn't come up with the idea, they said it was not a good idea and put a stop to it. Several years later, the sales rep from Cessna told Herman Brown the dumbest thing Cessna ever did was listen to that advice. Kirby could always draw a crowd. Kirby would have been the draw, not the airplanes, but the people would see all the new planes, and Cessna would have sold some.

Pilot Licensing

The Aero Club of America, described as an aircraft "social club" to promote aviation, began issuing pilot licenses in 1911. The Wright Brothers were among the first, as might be expected. U.S. Army, required Aero Club licenses for its pilots until 1914. But back then, pilot licenses were not mandatory. They were mostly for prestige and show.

Pilots were not licensed until the passage of the Air Commerce Act of 1926. The Aeronautics Branch was created by then Secretary of Commerce, Herbert Hoover. The agency carried out aviation regulatory responsibilities. The Airways Division was organized within the Bureau of Lighthouses.

The first actual pilot license was not issued until April 6, 1927. The first pilot to be licensed was William P. McCracken, Jr., then Assistant Secretary of Commerce for Aeronautics. Orville Wright declined the offer to be the first licensed pilot because he was no longer flying by that time.

It is often reported that Kirby Grant was an accomplished pilot in real life. Perhaps some of those reports grew out of air shows where Kirby was the show announcer. But Kirby may have contributed to those stories. On Good Morning America, Kirby and Gloria "Penny "Winters were interviewed by Charles Gibson. Gloria said that they both had pilot licenses, but that Kirby had lost his due to his medical condition after his heart surgery in 1978.

Gibson: "Now, who flew?"
Grant: "I did fly, and of course, she (Gloria) did also. "
Winters: "He was always handling things.."
Grant: "We had such marvelous people from the Cessna Corporation in Wichita to help us out, so some of that hairy flying, they made me look awful good..."
Gibson: "..but you really are a flyer..."
Grant: "Well, I did, up until I had open heart surgery, and of course, they took the ticket but I still do a little of it from the right-hand side."
Gibson went on to say, "It's fairly well established that Kirby Hoon, Jr. was rejected for pilot training during World War II because of color blindness."[2]

Don't believe everything you see on television.
You can find that interview on my Tim Trott Productions YouTube channel.

---

2. (Source: Good Morning America - Reunion show with Charles Gibson © ABC Television)

Kirby once said that he and two college friends had "learned how to fly" in a WACO aircraft from "barnstormers" in Montana in the 1920s. As we reported earlier, the WACO was a tail-wheel biplane built by the Weaver Aircraft Company. Kirby related a similar story about learning to fly in a WACO aircraft to aerobatic pilot Walter Pierce, whom we mentioned in the previous chapter.

There were many unsupported anecdotal reports of Grant flying airplanes at air shows.

As we know, in the flying scenes with the Cessna 310B, the pilot was Bill Fergusson. In an interview with Michael McMurtrey in August of 1996, Bill Fergusson said that when he was working with Kirby Grant, he "showed no interest in flying the airplane at all." (Source: Transcript from Michael McMurtrey used with permission)

Someone with first-hand knowledge told me of a time when Kirby was being flown in a Cessna 310 to an air show and was offered to take the controls. It's not that complicated to maintain a straight and level flight. That's the first thing a student pilot does. But Kirby declined the offer

Steven Brown related a time when he owned a 310, and a television station wanted to take some pictures. Steve had Kirby sit on the left (the pilot's seat), and when they did a low pass, Steve would bend down so the cameras couldn't see him. While they were flying around, Steven asked Kirby, "Do you want to fly this thing"? Kirby responded, "Well, I really don't know how to fly. When we were doing some of those picture shows, ...I did fly straight and level, stuff like that, a few times, but I never did take off and land it."

It has been reported that Kirby Grant's pilot's license was issued in 1929 and expired in 1978 for medical reasons. At the annual Oshkosh air show one year, one individual claimed that Kirby Grant held a pilot license under another "secret" name. The FAA does not do that. There are no records at Federal Aviation Administration of a pilot's license issued under the name Kirby Grant or his real name Kirby Grant Hoon, Jr.

Roy Rogers was a pilot and owned a Cessna Bobcat (the same model as the original Songbird), but his pilot license said Leonard Franklin Slye. Gene Autry flew as a USAF pilot, and his FAA license read *Orvon Grover Autry*. The FAA does not issue licenses under fictional names.

But there's another side to the story; when Kirby Grant did show an interest in actual flying. One source quoted Kip (Kirby Grant, III), saying that his father was a "real pilot". It sad that the two flew together many times. Kip and his sister, Kristen, told how their father took his kids flying on many occasions. Kip expressed a similar statement in my interview with him. When I asked how he could do that if he didn't have a license, he replied, "I didn't say he had a license..."

It certainly would not fit the character for Kirby Grant to fly without a license. I strongly suspect the "rest of the story" is that Kirby took a "real" pilot along for those trips. I have names, unconfirmed, of several Cessna 310 pilots who may have played that role for Kirby.

Licensed or not, Kirby Grant certainly did play the part of a pilot well on television. Well enough that he inspired many real pilots and astronauts, including five of the seven astronauts aboard STS-61-A. Those astronauts flew the last successful mission of the Space Shuttle Challenger.

I don't know how many doctors were inspired by TV doctors Welby or Kildare to join the medical profession. Still, I'm pretty sure they didn't expect Robert Young or Richard Chamberlain to have actual medical degrees.

As "Sky King," Kirby Grant had a significant impact on aviation that lasted long after the television show and the character he portrayed. In the eyes of many, that made him a "real pilot."

At the end of the book Sky King by Ron Muerke, there is a poem that ends with these lines:

> Many lives were touched by this TV man,
> and many of the pilots of today are pilots because of him
> We need a hero like him more now than we did then,
> but unfortunately, they quit making heroes like him
> (Jim Dilly)

"Sky King" was a true legend, and Kirby Grant was the inspiration to a generation of pilots who came "Out of the Blue."

If you enjoyed this book, please take a few moments to write a nice review where you purchased it and recommend it to your friends and social media followers!

About the Author

Tim Trott became interested in flying at an early age, watching the "Sky King " television program in front of a bulky, black and white console TV like so many others of that time. By coincidence, Tim later became acquainted with the actor who played the television role of Sky King, Kirby Grant Hoon, Jr., and his wife, Carolyn Grant, when the family retired to Florida in the early 1970s.

Aviation has played a small part in Tim's life from time to time through the years, from riding along with WLCY Radio's "Eye in the Sky" traffic reporter in Tampa Bay with "Capt." Dan Lunin, and from working for CE Avionics at Sanford Airport in the 1970s to his interest in UAVs ("drones") much later. Initially approved for a Section 333 drone exemption under part 91, he then earned a Remote Pilot Certification the first day it became available in August 2016. While logging a few dozen hours with sUAS aircraft, Tim has also logged a (very) few hours as a student pilot... in Cessna aircraft (naturally).

Growing out of the e-books, a video training series at TheDroneProfessor.com, and on-site lectures, has helped most of a thousand students to prepare for the FAA Remote Pilot Certification (RPC) exam.

Tim's other efforts include certification as an FDLE (Florida Department of Law Enforcement Cert #329775) instructor, teaching courses in the application, mission planning, operation, and safety of UAVs for public safety and first responders, as well as law enforcement response to "drone" complaints.

Tim is now or has been a member or associated with several aviation organizations, including APSA, AMA, AUVSI, EAA, FSANA, AOPA, and the FAA Safety Team.

Tim is also involved with hosting and designing websites and has used that experience to write *Guarding Against Online Identity Theft*, with a Spanish translation, in 2022. Now retired and living on Florida's East Coast and still staying with the non-fiction trend, *T is for Treason* traces the history of that topic from Benedict Arnold to the present day.

Tim Trott has always had a love for writing and teaching. His first writing for publication came in High School, reporting on a YMCA trip to Monterey, Mexico. They published those reports in the Orlando Sentinel. Fast forward to 2016, when his fascination with drones led to the purchase of a DJI Phantom 2 and writing about the experience in *The Droner's Guide*, which was replaced by the *FAA Remote Pilot Study Guide* a year later, and expanded to online training.

Please consider these other books by the author:

Biography: *Out of the Blue: The life and legend of Kirby "Sky King" Grant, First Through the Fire (Talbert Gray)*

Education: *Understanding WordPress 6.x for Beginners*

Security: *Guarding Against Online Identity Theft* and *Proteccion de Identidad*

Politics/History: *T is for Treason, Broken Border*

Science Fiction: *What If... (Vol 1)*

Misc/LCB: *LOTTO TRAKR*